SO YOU WANT
TO BE AN ACADEMIC
LIBRARY DIRECTOR

ALA Editions purchases fund advocacy, awareness,
and accreditation programs for library professionals worldwide.

SO YOU WANT TO BE AN ACADEMIC LIBRARY DIRECTOR

EDITED BY
COLLEEN S. HARRIS

An imprint of the American Library Association

CHICAGO   2017

COLLEEN S. HARRIS serves as information literacy coordinator and assistant librarian at the Broome Library on the California State University Channel Islands faculty. Previously, she served as head of access services at The University of Tennessee at Chattanooga, and as assistant head of access and delivery services at North Carolina State University. Harris received her MLS degree from the University of Kentucky, an MFA in writing from Spalding University (Louisville, Kentucky), and an EdD in learning & leadership from The University of Tennessee at Chattanooga. Her work has appeared as book chapters in *Library Management Tips That Work* (2011), *The Frugal Librarian* (2011), *Writing and Publishing: The Librarian's Handbook* (2010), and *Teaching Generation M: A Handbook for Librarians and Educators* (2009); and as articles in *Library Review, Journal of Access Services, The Bottom Line: Managing Library Finances,* and *Library Journal.* Harris also served as coeditor of the collection *Women on Poetry: Writing, Revising, Publishing and Teaching* (2012), and is a three-time Pushcart Prize nominee for her poetry and short fiction. Her research interests include academic library leadership and management, library instruction impacts on student learning, and applied research methods in academic settings.

© 2017 by the American Library Association

ISBN: 978-0-8389-1496-0 (paper)

Library of Congress Cataloging-in-Publication Data

Names: Harris, Colleen S., 1979- editor.
Title: So you want to be an academic library director / edited by Colleen S. Harris.
Description: Chicago : ALA Editions, an imprint of the American Library Association, 2017. |
    Includes bibliographical references and index.
Identifiers: LCCN 2017014841 | ISBN 9780838914960 (pbk. : alk. paper)
Subjects: LCSH: Academic library directors—Employment. | Academic libraries—Administration.
    | Academic library directors—United States—Employment. | Academic libraries—United
    States—Administration.
Classification: LCC Z682.4.A34 S65 2017 | DDC 025.1/977092—dc23 LC record available at
    https://lccn.loc.gov/2017014841

Text design in the Chaparral, Gotham, and Bell Gothic typefaces.

♾ This paper meets the requirements of ANSI/NISO Z39.48-1992 (Permanence of Paper).

Printed in the United States of America

21 20 19 18 17   5 4 3 2 1

Contents

Preface

IF YOU ARE A LIBRARY DIRECTOR, a department head, or a librarian with management aspirations, you have given some thought to the skills, knowledge, and characteristics that lead to success.

You might turn to a number of studies for guidance. These studies are useful because they aggregate a range of perspectives from surveys and find common attributes among them. The ability to envision a future and motivate staff to get there, to plan and budget, and to define problems and make decisions are a few examples of skills to cultivate. We know, of course, that library administrators have reached their positions by a variety of career paths. Recently collected data from midsized college and university library directors not only confirms this, but reveals that most academic library directors don't get to exercise necessary skills until they become directors. The reality is that while new academic library directors might be developing relationships and informing scholarly communities on the issues of the day, they are often distracted by the overwhelming work required to get up-to-speed on those necessary leadership skills.

Learning on the job is part of working life, even for directors. To complement the formal research on academic library directors' characteristics, I have recruited library directors to write essays reflecting on various aspects of their work as library directors.

Peter Drucker once said (and many have repeated), "Culture eats strategy for breakfast," and so we start there, while finding our way to strategy as well. Among the topics our contributors address are library emergency planning, combating impostors'syndrome, the legal constraints in dealing with a recalcitrant employee, shared governance and multi-institutional collaboration, and cultural programming that challenges biases.

Each of the chapters in this book will give you a glimpse of the work of an academic library director and touch on areas you may not have thought of. We hope that together they will help you see where you may best apply your strengths, hone your skills, and plan your career.

PEG SEIDEN and
ELEANOR MITCHELL

1
Navigating Institutional Culture

Building Bridges and Not Burning Them

COLLEGES AND UNIVERSITIES possess their own institutional cultures and political climates, as do the libraries within them. As a new library director, developing an understanding of your institution may be the single most important factor in your success. Your professional expertise, for example your knowledge of personnel management, of budgeting, and even your vision of the future of libraries will not hold sway if you are unable to navigate your institutional culture. The development of a good understanding of an institution, its politics and culture is something that happens over time—years, in fact. Unlike other areas of management, there is no curriculum that directly addresses the skills that enable you to deftly navigate your institutional environment. What you can do is to hone the skills that create heightened awareness of the institutional dynamic and prepare you to work within it.

Essentially, this chapter addresses what is known in the literature as "workplace politics." The political environment is the result of the way numerous factors come together: organizational or institutional culture; governance structures (formal political systems); and the personalities of the individuals who wield varying amounts of power within the institution. As administrator of the library, the director has multiple cultural layers to navigate: that of the leadership culture of peers and supervisor (vice president, dean, provost, etc.), the library culture, and the college or university culture, as well as the faculty and student cultures.

What do you need to pay attention to in order to thrive in your political environment? How are decisions made; who are the power brokers; and what is the perceived value of the library on campus? This chapter will provide you with an *overview of the elements* that comprise an institution's culture and politics. These include a discussion of both formal and informal structures within and outside the library and strategies to help you succeed in your position as a key administrator.

FRAMING THE DISCUSSION

Many disciplines such as sociology, organizational psychology, and management have studied workplace culture and politics. For the purposes of this chapter, the authors have focused on the literature of higher education and librarianship as being most relevant to the topic at hand. Much of the literature on this topic falls into the arena of advice or professional development. Here we note selected materials from this perspective, while referring to some of the seminal scholarship in the field for context.

Institutional or organizational culture as manifested in the workplace was explored in a systematic manner as early as the 1920s and 1930s, with the Hawthorne studies at the Western Electric Company. Intended to look at how physical working conditions could impact productivity, "Hawthorne set the individual in a social context, establishing that the performance of employees is influenced by their surroundings and by the people that they are working with as much as by their own innate abilities."[1] A now widely accepted definition of this concept was offered by Edgar Schein who, in his seminal book on the topic of organizational culture, described culture as "a pattern of shared basic assumptions learned by a group as it solved its problems of external adaptation and internal integration, that has worked well enough to be considered valid and, therefore, to be taught to new members as the correct way to perceive, think, and feel in relation to those problems."[2] Schein enumerates the observable events and forces that comprise group culture: behavioral regularities when people interact (such as language, customs, traditions, and rituals), group norms, espoused values, formal philosophy, rules of the game (or "the way we do it here"), climate, embedded skills (such as unwritten procedures), habits of thinking or mental models, shared meanings, root metaphors (how groups characterize themselves), and rituals and celebrations.[3] In a 2013 article featured on the *Harvard Business Review* website, Michael

Watkins distilled a conversation he facilitated through LinkedIn into a hand-ful of principles that further illuminate the hard-to-define concept of insti-tutional culture. Among the characteristics of culture he notes the following: "Culture is a process of 'sense-making' in organizations. . . . Culture is a carrier of meaning. Cultures provide a shared view not only of 'what is' but also of 'why is.'"[4]

A method called the competing values framework (CVF) was developed in 1983 by Rohrbaugh and Quinn, presenting a model for organizing crite-ria used to evaluate organizational effectiveness;[5] Cameron and Quinn's 2006 book presents a strategy, instruments, and methodology for applying this model.[6] This approach has been adopted by academic libraries in efforts to better understand organizational culture. In their 2004 article entitled "Orga-nizational Cultures of Libraries as a Strategic Resource," Kaarst-Brown et al. consider whether there are aspects of organizational culture in libraries that can be key to personal and organizational success,[7] using the competing val-ues framework as a method to reveal and examine these characteristics.

The literature review will continue with a discussion of workplace politics particularly with respect to the higher education environment and libraries.

LEARNING ABOUT THE INSTITUTION AND ITS FORMAL AND INFORMAL POWER STRUCTURES

Power structures in institutions of higher education are realized both through informal and formal governance and organizational structures. Colleges and universities generally have similar governance structures, with some variation depending upon affiliation (public or private) and size. For example, institu-tions will have a governing board, whose members may be called trustees, regents, governors, or managers. Other major players in the governance of a college or university are senior administrators (president, chancellor, and var-ious vice presidents) and, of course, the faculty. The library director needs to understand where he or she fits within this structure. You may be on the pres-ident's staff or report to someone on the president's staff. You may also partic-ipate in specific leadership groups on campus such as the dean's or directors' group. In addition, library directors may be key members of cross-campus standing committees that focus on critical or infrastructural issues. Member-ships and roles may vary depending on whether the library director is a faculty member or an administrator or whether there is a staff or faculty union.

On many campuses, committees are responsible for setting the institu-tion's strategic agenda and making decisions about core issues as wide-ranging as benefits, budget, or the academic program. It's important that the library director be aware of the relative status and power of these committees. By vir-tue of their position, the library director may be required to serve on specific committees, such as the curriculum or educational policy committees. But even if she is not on a committee, she should be aware of their agendas. Even committees with no direct library connection may on occasion consider topics that impact the library. On many campuses there is a library committee or, in some cases, a joint library and information technology committee. The role of these committees can vary from simply advisory to advocacy, as can their influence. Sometimes, faculty members with the least power or influence end up on these committees. If the library director is asked to make recommendations, much thought should be given to the composition of the committee. There may be a stipulation that all divisions of the institution are represented on the library committee, but within that structure the selection of members provides an opportunity to build the strongest committee possible. If your agenda for the library is progressive, beware of the tendency for the appointments committee to appoint only bibliophiles. Look for those who see the library as more than a book box or buying club, those that recognize the library's expansive role.

The governance structures may be documented in the handbook, catalog, or on the website for the institution. Another glimpse into the institution's political and cultural framework may be provided by the strategic plan, accreditation documents, or self-studies. These documents will articulate the vision and priorities for the campus and provide the new director with a road map to follow in developing the library's program.

Informal structures extend well beyond the governance and administrative structures of the institution. They are often based on individual relationships and personalities. For example, a particular faculty member may hold undue influence because of a friendship with the president or other senior administrator; this power may wane with a change of administration. Or an individual may be very vocal and may have the support of a small but influential group of colleagues; this can give that individual's voice more authority on campus matters well beyond his own department.

The new library director will be hard-pressed to find any documentation of these power structures, nor are they likely to be immediately visible. They have generally evolved over time and are deeply embedded in the institution's culture. The best way to understand these structures and how to operate within them is in conversation with your supervisor. You may ask him to suggest key faculty and administrators that you might talk to about the institution. Identifying faculty members with strong opinions about the library should also be among your first priorities. These may be committee chairs, senior faculty, or just individuals with history or an agenda.

These informal structures are intertwined with the more formal structures and together they influence the way the institution operates and how information flows within the institution. A key characteristic that defines how these structures work together is the specific institution's shared governance model. In almost all institutions of higher education, power is shared by the faculty, senior administration, and governing board, though the actual balance of power is determined by institutional culture, history, and personalities and may shift over time. The decision-making role and amount of power that any of the major players in an institution's governance structure wield relates to the issues at hand and can vary depending on the institution. It can also vary depending on the culture of the institution: is this a top-down, more authoritative culture or is it a more consensus-building one?

One of the overarching factors that determines the library's role in governance is whether the librarians are considered faculty. If librarians have faculty status, this may put them in a different power dynamic vis-à-vis librarians who are considered "staff" or "administrators." Another factor that affects the authority of the library is where it sits in the institution's organizational structure. While most academic library directors traditionally reported to the chief academic officer such as the provost or dean of faculty, in new models and merged organizations, the library may be placed in the information technology unit and thus report to a chief information officer. In other institutions, the library director works under the supervision of an associate provost, rather than the provost.

EFFECTIVENESS IN THE INSTITUTIONAL ENVIRONMENT

The library's ability to achieve its objectives is dependent on its perceived value to the institution and its relationship to the rest of the community. In developing relationships with the community, the library director should be cognizant that not all of the library's friends and supporters may be equally influential. Power on many campuses is tied to funding through tuition dollars and grants, and the library's traditional advocates (the humanists and humanistic social scientists) have diminished power on many campuses as career-focused and STEM (science, technology, engineering, and math) curricula ascend in importance.

Even though the library may have a cadre of supporters, when it comes to the budget no one is going to fight the library's fight. In order to achieve the library's programmatic goals, you will be in competition for dollars with every academic and administrative department head. You may see the library as a common good and think that everyone will be looking out for the library, but everyone is vying for the same small piece of a pie. The context in which the annual budget process takes place is formal but is subject to informal pressures. In establishing the campus budget, the institution may be subject to parameters set by state government and/or the governing board. Usually strategic priorities for the campus will guide the budget decisions, although these may be overridden by crisis or opportunity (for example, the Great Recession of 2008). In most situations, the library administration will prepare an initial budget proposal, but the formal budget approval process will vary from institution to institution. Budget advocacy may be bolstered by alliances that are part of the institution's informal political structures and relationships. Sometimes the library director's political capital may be insufficient to advocate by herself, and these strategic alliances then become critical to realizing the library's programmatic goals.

Even where the library's practices and processes are determined internally, the broader campus community informs those strategies. For example, collections are built in response to curricular and scholarly direction, and the information literacy program relies on collaboration with faculty. Library goals related to areas like open access, digital scholarship, records management, and preservation must be "owned" by the campus, and cannot be pursued or achieved without broader support.

Dealing with Conflict

As a new library director, you must learn to navigate around various flashpoints and land mines, some of which may be very specific to the institution. These often have to do with the emotional attachments that faculty, in particular, have to library spaces, collections, and personnel. These emotional attachments are sometimes related to symbolic value that connotes prestige and power, such as having a branch library in a department or a designated bibliographer or subject specialist. They may be things you can anticipate—for example, a reaction against a plan to move print off campus to a storage facility; they may be unexpected, such as a heated response to a plan to remove the reference desk and move to a consultation model. Often the library director is caught between a rock and hard place. Senior administration may ask the director to save money or reallocate space while faculty may have very different priorities. Added to the mix are the director's own desires to implement best practices which may not align with either administrative directives or faculty preferences.

Whether the library director is an administrator or faculty member will affect how she is able to act in the environment, particularly when there may be significant distrust between the faculty and the administration. There is often a risk of alienating one group or another. If you alienate faculty, it may be difficult to rely upon them for support subsequently. For example, in times of financial exigency, the library director may be the "team player" whose decisions help the campus weather difficult periods; these decisions could potentially compromise the relationship with faculty if they call for subscription cancellations or scaling back library hours. But if you alienate your administration, though you may occupy the moral high ground you may risk severe consequences. For instance, there have been cases where library directors have lost their jobs by sticking to their principles in the face of administrative disapproval. Sometimes these conflicts revolve around organizational structure—such as a campus imperative to merge the library with the information technology area; at other times they may be about relocating or removing collections to free up library space for other campus needs, or about the pace and practicality of technological change. Much depends upon the relative power of the administration and faculty on your campus and whose team you are perceived to be on.

Many of the potential land mines derive from the changing nature of the academic library. For example, there are generational and disciplinary differences in expectations among faculty. Newly minted PhDs may come from R1 institutions where the relationship with the library around research support and collections may differ from that of a smaller, liberal arts college. One might find that a new faculty member in media studies has certain expectations about the library's role in digital scholarship. A senior member of the economics department may have a reliance on the digital environment for data sources and journal articles that might seem foreign to a historian whose research depends on access to monographs or physical archives. One can't assume that the pace at which the library moves to digital or new support models will be as comfortable for the former as the latter. People may also be uncomfortable with the shift away from a model of preemptively building collections to one that is premised on pay-per-view, where there is no longer an emphasis on developing the resources for posterity. Any decisions emanating from the library may be called into question by one group or another if those decisions conflict with their perspective on what the role of the library should be.

A key area of potential conflict relates to the way in which library space is utilized. In many libraries, space for collections is being reallocated to other purposes. Some of these purposes are consonant with the library's traditional functions, for example, classrooms and new kinds of study or work spaces. In other cases the square footage of the library is viewed as up for grabs for less closely related purposes. Libraries may be asked to find space for student support services, or information technologists, or completely unrelated functional offices. The library director needs to both respond to and define the appropriate role of the physical building. Is it primarily the center for student academic life, a social space, a place for cultural activities, or is it perceived as a place limited to scholarly pursuits and the collections that support them?

How does one navigate these potential areas of conflict? The director can learn the hard way, by attempting to implement change and running headlong into a conflict. It is preferable to develop an early warning system that avoids these snafus before they happen, by establishing ongoing communication mechanisms that inform about campus issues and priorities as well as emerging or immediate concerns. The best approach is to make connections with the broader college community both through informal (inviting them for coffee) and formal means (committee work). Secondly, one should be able to capitalize on existing connections that library staff have, with the caveat that the director should not draw these staff into the conflict. Most libraries will have a formal outreach structure that has people "on the ground" who are listening to the campus at large—that is, librarians who support different academic departments and cocurricular areas. Yet one cannot necessarily count on these librarians to identify and negotiate areas of possible conflict. For instance, the subject librarians need to be able to retain strong positive relationships with their faculty and may be reluctant to engage with faculty on sensitive issues. However, the library director should have a mechanism for gathering this "intelligence" from staff members. In addition, the senior staff member to whom the library director reports has yet broader access to conversations and decisions at higher levels, which can provide both perspective and specifics to inform the director. If you are fortunate, your senior staff member can be a wonderful partner with whom to jointly solve problems.

Building Your Street Credibility

In order to enhance your success as the library director you need to build credibility within the broader community. The strongest element in building your credibility is the quality of your work, which is reflected in the quality of library services and resources. The library director gets reflected glory or blame from every interaction that the community has with the library. Comments from faculty, students, or administrators may praise the collection, or the miraculous powers of interlibrary loan staff, or the impact of an information literacy session. These statements attest to the value of the library and establish the credibility of the director on the campus. The director's participation in campuswide committees also can influence people's perception of him or her. Beyond speaking on library-related issues, the director's thoughtful engagement with broader campus issues under the committee's consideration can solidify his or her reputation. The director's professional profile and visibility in librarianship or another academic discipline can also assist in building credibility, particularly among other administrators and faculty. Through publications, conference presentations, or professional association work, the library director can establish his external bona fides which often are seen by campus colleagues as signs of professional credibility.

Your effectiveness as a library director will depend on the relationships you develop within the formal and informal power structures. Perhaps the best approach is to build alliances with individuals and departments whose interests align with and who can support the library's mission and priorities. For example, there are a number of libraries that have developed and promoted open-access resolutions on their campuses. Those libraries that have been successful in passing such a resolution have typically identified a champion on the faculty. This is usually someone who has not only demonstrated interest in the topic, but has credibility with his or her colleagues. Beyond faculty, there are numerous other natural partners that the library director should reach out to. One might think first of information technology (IT) services because of overlapping interests in instructional technology and information management. While some level of IT support will certainly be structural in your organization, to develop partnerships and an expansive system of collaboration, it is beneficial for the library director to establish informal connections with key personnel. There may be other relationships that derive from shared space with units like student support services or writing centers. Even when these services are not located in the library, it behooves the library director to seek out her peers in these areas because of mutual concerns around teaching, learning, and scholarship. One can find examples of successful partnerships between academic libraries and many different campus entities including career services, development, alumni affairs, finance, intercultural or diversity initiatives, the dean of students' office, service learning initiatives, communications, admissions, human resources, institutional research, and the art gallery. For example, some libraries work with alumni affairs to extend access to online databases. Others work with departments such as admissions to host prospective students when they visit campus. Libraries work regularly with institutional research on national statistical surveys but also reach out to them for expertise on developing surveys and focus groups, as well as institutional review board approval. Some of these partnerships are episodic, but others are essential to the health of the library and should be sustained over time. By virtue of the core responsibilities of the library, the director will have ongoing relationships with offices such as finance, facilities, and human resources. Positive campus relationships enhance library visibility and build political capital which is there when you need it.

LEADING THE LIBRARY

When you arrive as a new library director (with your own baggage), it is important to know that the library staff also has history and baggage, and each of you will bring that to every encounter you have. There may be a honeymoon period, but you will certainly be held up in contrast (positively or negatively) to the previous director. Nevertheless, staff don't want to be compared to your previous staff, and the sooner that the new director moves beyond "the way we did it in my old library," the sooner the staff and director will bond and become a strong unit. The director's credibility within the library, among library staff, is dependent upon the local organizational culture; staff, however, need to see consistency and transparency in your decision-making so that they can develop a sense of trust in you.

Power in the library is really about the responsibility, explicit or tacit, for making decisions. Power in the library should ideally align with the organizational structure. But there are likely to be individuals who wield power outside of that structure, whose activities can ensnare the unwary director. For example, in institutions with faculty status, librarians with greater longevity and rank can challenge or even undermine the new director. Or there may be preexisting relationships—friendships, even marriages—between library staff and campus administrators or faculty which may create back channels of information and opinion that may impact the library. The director needs to be alert to symptoms that this might be happening, noting, for example, particular resistance, morale issues, or rumors from outside the library. In the same way that you build alliances outside the library, you need to build them within it. The library director cannot assume that trust with each member of the staff is automatic. He or she must work to build that trust by listening, ensuring that each staff member feels enfranchised and providing them with opportunities for engagement and leadership.

Meetings are one of the places where the power dynamics play out. Who gets included in meetings and why? By sitting at the table, one gets to have input into and influence over decisions; one hears information more directly and immediately, and has unfiltered access to opinions and perceptions. One also has an opportunity to shape the disseminated message. The new library director should understand the local meeting culture. Is there a tradition of broad inclusivity that cuts across staff at all levels, or does the library have a more segregated culture wherein only staff of a certain status are included in the key decision-making groups?

The new director should be aware of how communication happens or flows within and among staff members, beyond the structure of scheduled meetings. There are informal avenues of communication that are likely already in place: note who talks to whom, who has coffee with whom, who socializes outside of the library. The library director is often outside the library's informal social sphere, and will not have the same opportunities to develop relationships and communicate casually and informally with the staff. Thus the director may not be privy to the informal discussions about library issues and topics that will play out within meetings. To counterbalance what can be unproductive informal communication paths, the library director should ensure that there are sufficient formal mechanisms that provide staff with the opportunity to be enfranchised, be well informed, and participate in the conversation about the library's future. It also behooves the library director, as a participant in multiple campus forums and as someone privy to information from different venues, to provide library staff with perspective and help them make the connections. The library director may be caught between a rock and a hard place. Sometimes staff opinions may run counter to the position of the library director when it comes to reconciling campus needs with library priorities. The library director runs the risk of alienating staff in order to seemingly appease campus interests. The staff may not recognize that there is a larger benefit that accrues to the library (often in terms of political capital) in making unpopular decisions. The library director has to weigh competing interests and potential consequences. While the library is your arena, your decisions are made in the context of institution-wide priorities and values.

STRATEGIES FOR YOUR SUCCESS

What are the strategies that will help you navigate your new institution's culture? A first priority is to find the professional communities that will provide you with ongoing support and wisdom. As the lone library director at your institution, it will be invaluable for you to develop a network of similarly placed professionals to help you navigate through your environment. Professional development experiences, such as workshops on leadership techniques, team building, and problem resolution will also be helpful. While these strategies can provide you with a mentor outside the institution who understands your position and responsibilities, it is critical to also find at least one mentor within the institution who understands its culture and politics. Your local mentor will help you get to know the institution, but there are other strategies that can also further your understanding and help you build a deeper political awareness that will serve you in your role as director.

> Identify and connect with your peer colleagues across the institution. You may be part of a formal group such as a dean's council that meets regularly. If not, with careful deliberation seek out those at your level who have great respect on campus.

> Build partnerships and develop alliances with administrative departments. There may be obvious partners such as student support services, the writing center, and IT, but be wary that your overtures to any particular partner do not create turf wars.

> Cultivate strong relationships with the academic program. Developing relationships with key faculty is critically important, but you should not overlook opportunities to forge connections with the administrative assistants in academic departments. They provide

a different but very necessary perspective on their faculty and the priority issues for their departments.

Don't forget your primary clientele, the students. It may be helpful to form a student advisory group if one doesn't already exist. Talk to your student workers; learn from them what they and their peers think about the library.

Cultivate informal chains of communication; capitalize on informal networks. While the strategies previously mentioned focus on formal relationships, you often have the opportunity to develop informal relationships with faculty, staff, and administrators through outside activities. Do you know who is in your bike group or yoga class?

Ensure a good level of visibility on campus; become part of the campus community. While work/life balance is necessary, the director should try to attend major campus events, as well as departmental events such as lectures and performances. This doesn't need to be burdensome; find those activities that align with your personal interest, whether they are music, dance, art, politics, or the environment.

Keep up with institutional politics, including the rumor mill; various campus constituencies have differing issues. Read the student newspaper and social media sites regularly to find out hot-button topics for the students. Read faculty blogs; you might even "friend" some faculty on Facebook. Hang out at the coffee bar; see who's having lunch and join them. The talk will inevitably turn to campus concerns.

Learn what the tone is and adapt your style; calibrate your behavior to what's effective in the institutional culture. Be judicious and restrained; or be the squeaky wheel. Particularly as a new director trying to introduce change, you will find more success and less frustration if you both know the local process and acknowledge the campus culture in your approach. Some institutions are more entrepreneurial and seek out change agents; others may be more conservative and rest heavily on traditions.

Within the library, the director has a great deal of power and influence; you need to be cognizant of the impact of even your most casual comments on the staff, particularly as they are learning your style. Depending on the style of the previous director, staff may be more comfortable with "taking direction" than with a more participatory management approach. If you seek the "wisdom of the crowd" in your own management style, you need to be completely up-front with your expectations of the staff. Let staff know that it is okay to disagree; actively model dissent.

Capitalize on your honeymoon period; go for the big wins; ask the naive questions. Although people will be watching you closely and, frankly, judging you, this is probably the one time you will be granted leniency for mistakes you are likely to make. Understand that no matter how long you are with an institution, you will continue to make mistakes and misread situations. A great director knows how to recoup from her losses and move on.

NOTES

1. "The Hawthorne Effect," *The Economist*, November 3, 2008, adapted from *The Economist Guide to Management Ideas and Gurus*, by Tim Hindle (Profile Books), www.economist.com/node/12510632.

2. Edgar H. Schein, *Organizational Culture and Leadership* (San Francisco: Jossey-Bass, 2010).

3. Ibid.

4. Michael Watkins, "What Is Institutional Culture? And Why Should We Care?" *Harvard Business Review*, May 15, 2013, https://hbr.org/2013/05/what-is-organizational-culture/.

5. Robert E. Quinn, and J. Rohrbaugh, "A Spatial Model of Effectiveness Criteria: Towards a Competing Values Approach to Organizational Analysis," *Management Science* 29, no. 3 (1983): 363–77.

6. Kim Cameron and Robert E. Quinn, *Diagnosing and Changing Organizational Culture: Based on the Competing Values Framework* (San Francisco: Jossey-Bass, 2006).

7. Michelle L. Kaarst-Brown, Scott Nicholson, Gisela M. von Dran, and Jeffrey M. Stanton, "Organizational Cultures of Libraries as a Strategic Resource," *Library Trends* 53, no. 1 (2004): 33–53.

2
The Art of Asking

Communicating Expectations within Your Library

LIKE MANY LIBRARIANS, I enjoy TED Talks, short presentations recorded at the Technology/Entertainment/Design Conferences that have become very popular venues for sharing new ideas and fostering conversation. These digestible nuggets of wisdom can be easily absorbed while wolfing down my lunch in my office, and they often give me food for thought as well. One of my favorites is "The Art of Asking" by Amanda Palmer, a somewhat controversial musician and artist (Palmer, 2013). Ostensibly targeted at art and music, she asks that rather than adopting digital rights management or other technological methods to oppose piracy, we examine instead how we can ask people to pay for artistic endeavors. As the head of one of the most successful Kickstarter campaigns, Palmer can be said to be a guru in the art of asking. She followed up her TED Talk with a best-selling book in which she expanded on the concept and touched further on how she excels at asking—and where she still needs to work (Palmer, 2014).

After reading the book, I decided to present a session at my state library association conference on the "Art of Asking for Library Workers." The session description said, in part, that "attendees will develop ideas, via lively discussion with colleagues, on how to ask for what they need and want for (and from!) their communities, with an emphasis on crowdsourcing." However, in the actual session, during that lively discussion, we found that almost all of our concerns in asking dealt with internal library issues—how to delegate, how to get clarification from our employers or boards, and how to feel confident in our jobs. The room was filled primarily with librarians who headed up their own libraries, and I was surprised that the conversation had taken such a turn. A large part of my surprise stemmed from the now-disproved feeling that I was the only library director with these issues!

Asking for what we need can be the hardest aspect of any leadership role. When faced with delegating a task, for example, many new directors may instinctively choose to do the work themselves rather than ask a more appropriate person. Even when a task has been delegated directors may have problems with the resulting product, not receiving what they needed when it was needed. Furthermore, when library employees do not have a clear picture of expectations they cannot work effectively, which leads to their own frustrations with the workplace. Learning why, when, and how to ask makes communicating expectations much easier, and also helps us answer the questions of what and who to ask.

COMBATING IMPOSTOR SYNDROME

I run a small community college library. I and my staff of three individuals work with our campus's 2,000 students and over 100 faculty, mostly adjuncts. My campus is affiliated with a larger university in town and one of my employees, a quarter-time adjunct, is actually supervised by a librarian in their library with whom I interact only a couple times a year. This has offered some unique challenges in asking that employee for what I need in order to ensure the smooth running of my library. This is on top of the already-challenging need to delegate to and manage the two employees who officially report to me. However the reporting-line structure looks, the fact remains that I am in charge of this library and those who work here expect me to lay out what needs to be done and who is responsible for getting it done.

The first step for me was to discover why to ask. For many of us, as hinted at during the discussion at my conference session, we need to deal with why we think we cannot ask our employees or others impacted by our position for what we need. This can be part of the psychological phenomenon known as impostor syndrome. The feeling that we should not have whatever power we have been granted is endemic to librarianship, particularly academic librarianship where I work. We often feel like frauds who are on the verge of being called out and shamed, and this feeling more than anything else may keep us from delegating work effectively within our libraries. Those who are newer to the profession or are in positions new to them are more likely to suffer from impostor syndrome (Clark, Vardeman, and Barba, 2014, 265).

Some ways of dealing with these feelings are to keep in mind that feelings are not necessarily reflective of reality. Review your qualifications and seek positive feedback from your supervisor or from colleagues outside of your institution. Keep a log of compliments and praise to refer to when feelings of inadequacy arise. Seek out professional training in areas where you honestly feel you have a lack, and seek out professional help in the form of therapy if you have a difficult time feeling like you belong in your job (Clark, Vardeman, and Barba, 2014, 266).

Impostor syndrome, while especially common in the first few months of a new position, needs to be dealt with swiftly because if you get into a habit of doing work yourself, it will be harder to break. It is much more challenging to delegate work when we feel we lack the authority to do so, and it is hard to effectively communicate expectations when you feel you do not have the right to expect work from other people. These concerns often lead library workers suffering from impostor syndrome to avoid delegating work or explaining their expectations well.

Beyond your own possible feelings of inadequacy, it is important to foster a workplace environment that combats impostor syndrome in your employees. One of the contributing factors of impostor syndrome is unclear expectations from supervisors, and a chief way to address this is through positive and constructive criticism (Clark, Vardeman, and Barba, 2014, 266). If employees feel confident that they belong in their role and get good feedback on what they are doing right as well as wrong, the workplace will be healthier and more productive. Trust will increase on all sides, and delegation of work will be easier. This is another reason why we need to ask for our expectations as supervisors to be met, hard though it may be—it improves communication all around.

TRANSPARENCY AND PARTICIPATION

Fortunately, fostering a positive and constructive work environment also provides a good foundation for transparency and openness. If you feel confident in your role as a manager and are able to assign tasks to others in a direct and comprehensive way, and your workers feel empowered to carry out their assignments and ask for needed clarification, the entire workplace functions more smoothly. This type of workplace allows for everyone involved to ask and answer as situations arise.

This sort of workplace does not just happen. It requires a certain level of mindfulness and attention from the supervisor. In particular, a strong vision and shared goals for the workplace foster transparency and openness, and a good manager makes sure that what is being asked of employees ties in clearly with the aims of the workplace. Usually libraries, as service and knowledge-building community organizations, attract people who enjoy helping others and are looking to contribute to something larger than themselves. Making that connection clear in everything a worker does gives employees something to buy into, and a motivating connection to a larger whole. This gives us some insight into how we can ask for what we need from our employees.

For me, I addressed both my burgeoning impostor syndrome and the need to establish and communicate connection by participating in strategic-planning activities on my primary campus soon after I took my new position. As a branch library, we were free to take part in the main library's planning process if we desired, or not. Despite my fears that I was not really part of "the team," I spoke up early and often about my library's need to be part of the main library's strategic planning process and found myself appointed to a high-level committee drafting the main library's mission and plan. When that plan was complete, I could have returned to my branch library satisfied that I had put in some effort on the main campus, but instead I further carried the plan through to our library and our campus, creating with my team our own plan and goals based on the larger institution's, but targeted at our unique needs. These actions showed me first of all that it does not hurt to speak up and do some extra work, and that the connections that I fostered could be carried forward to my campus to inform our work and make us feel like part of a larger whole when we historically had felt neglected and ignored.

Our own awareness of how our institutions' work, from top to bottom, supports a larger enterprise makes it easier for us to ask for what we need from our employees. It is not just us as managers who are asking. It is also the library as an organization, and the community to which the library belongs. This structure helps us all see the boundaries of our work, and motivates us to respond. In addition, this awareness makes it easier for us to affirm with employees what works well and offer constructive criticism. It helps to remove the manager's ego from the process.

Knowing the big-picture view can also help us know what to ask. Sometimes a challenge in communicating expectations about tasks or roles simply involves knowing what our expectations ought to be. Understanding the overarching factors at play helps us see where our tasks as a library fit in. Then we can begin the occasionally difficult work of breaking these library wide tasks and goals down into actionable pieces. Part of the frustration both with asking for help and with offering help is the inability to see what the first step might be or how that step will fit in with the larger goal. In order to combat this, practice breaking down goals into manageable pieces that are actionable; that is, something which can be done. Writing a proposal investigating SMS/text message reference system options is a more actionable task for most of us than actually implementing an SMS reference system, but it still moves the library toward the goal.

KNOWING WHAT SUCCESS LOOKS LIKE

Another key part of communicating expectations is knowing what success looks like, and communicating that part to our employees. This helps employees "get it right," one of the bigger challenges of asking for help. If we let our employees know what the successful outcome of an assignment would be, this helps them feel more confident in getting there, and lets them meet our expectations better. A key part in this is making sure the things we ask for have a measurable outcome. Returning to the SMS reference service example, you could ask your employees to implement one, but if you give them some metrics such as cost, accessibility requirements, ease of staffing, and so on, you are far more likely to get what you wanted.

THE WHEN OF ASKING

Breaking what you are asking for down into more discrete and connected parts helps you figure out when it is appropriate to ask. Timeliness is important. You need to give the person you are asking for help a reasonable amount of time to do the task, but not so much time that the task feels unimportant. Clear deadlines also help with expectations—if you are asking for something specific and measurable as we have discussed, you will also want a particular time for its delivery. This helps your employees know where and how to prioritize tasks and what to devote their time to. People truly do like deadlines when they are done right, with an awareness of other work demands and a tie to the larger picture.

An example of this is the well-structured and surprisingly painless strategic planning process I participated in. The main library paid for an outside consultant, and part of her job was to break down this large task into discrete tasks with deadlines. This, in turn, made our work feel manageable and showed us how our small tasks built toward the larger whole. She also helped us clarify a vision for the plan that helped us see how what we were working on individually and collectively contributed to moving the library forward. This experience was so inspirational that it led me to conduct a mini-version of it within my own library as mentioned above, mostly because it felt doable and valuable.

WHO TO ASK

Sometimes the hardest part of asking for help is knowing who to ask. A manager skilled in the art of asking will know her employee's roles well, and will seek to clarify those roles with the employee. It is important to know if the employee's position description on paper matches up with what the employee actually does. A good knowledge of roles and actual work also helps us find areas of flux that may be open to change, and ask our employees to do work appropriate to their real jobs.

Keeping aware of workers' interests and areas of desired growth can also help with asking. New tasks may find allies and advocates among your staff in these interest areas, which will help you find the right person to connect with when new opportunities come up. As a manager, your involvement in the workplace lives of your employees on this level is not only a great tool for delegation, but an excellent way to build partnership toward the institution's vision and shared goals and further foster a positive and constructive work environment. Along these lines, be sure to reconfirm regularly with your staff the understanding of the library's vision and goals and their own individual part within the library mission.

My engagement of my branch library in the main library's strategic planning process spurred me to learn more about what my employees do, and want to do, on a day-to-day basis. It was one of the first projects I undertook as a manager that required me to really interact with my employees' desires for the future of our library and their own jobs, and thus spurred me to do well. While on paper I understood my role and my employees' roles well, in our discussions I learned far more about what I could ask of my employees and how to best do so.

Many managers and leaders are made by the ability to communicate expectations well. The key to doing so is through excellent and open communication generally, and by being brave enough to ask. I hope I will always remember my roomful of experienced library leaders, discussing the hard and vulnerable issues around asking for help, and I will keep in mind that I am not alone in feeling challenged within the profession. The art of asking is one that must be consistently practiced and is one where there likely will always be room for improvement.

BIBLIOGRAPHY

Clark, Melanie, Kimberly Vardeman, and Shelley Barba. 2014. "Perceived Inadequacy: A Study of the Imposter Phenomenon among College and Research Librarians." *College & Research Libraries* 75, no. 3 (May): 255–71.

Palmer, Amanda. "Amanda Palmer: The Art of Asking." 2013. TED video, 13:47. https://www.ted.com/talks/amanda_palmer_the_art_of_asking?language=en.

———. *The Art of Asking: How I Learned to Stop Worrying and Let People Help*. 2014. New York: Hachette.

PATRICIA S. BANACH

3

Collaboration in Connecticut Public Higher Education Libraries

MANAGING AND ENCOURAGING CHANGE are quite often a test of leadership, since most people prefer the comfort of the status quo. When the change is confined to a single institution, generally there is a mandate or authority to implement the change, and the well-known culture and environment of that institution affords a context for the proposed changes. However, when the change impacts multiple institutions with different missions and different cultures, the challenges are multiplied.

Such is the case with the Connecticut system of higher education, which was reorganized through an act of the Connecticut state legislature in 2011 and gave birth to the Connecticut State Colleges and Universities (CSCU) under the new Board of Regents for Higher Education beginning January 1, 2012. The institutions united in this new system are the four Connecticut State Universities (CSU),[1] the twelve community colleges,[2] and the online Charter Oak State College. The Connecticut State Library, though not under the Board of Regents, is also a key member of the library consortium by virtue of its long-standing participation in the CSU's shared library OPAC

(CONSULS). (The University of Connecticut is not part of this system and has its own Board of Trustees.)

At the campus level of the seventeen institutions there were varying degrees of enthusiasm or lack thereof (mostly the latter) for this merger. In this regard the merger may be considered a shotgun marriage championed by the newly elected governor of the state of Connecticut. Among the libraries of the system, however, there was a sense that this merger might provide an opportunity for meaningful collaboration, building on the traditional ethos of sharing common to libraries. While "a match made in heaven" is a phrase that describes our aspirations, achieving that match was still daunting.

The first leadership challenge was bringing the two groups of libraries together for the first time. Both groups had a history of very independent coexistence. There was the usual history of interlibrary loan, and there had been efforts at extending library privileges at some of the universities to some geographically close community colleges, but that was the extent of collaboration to that point. The community college library directors and the university library directors had never held a joint meeting. Some knew each other casually through the occasional encounter at a monthly meeting of the Council of Connecticut Academic Library Directors (all public and private academic library directors in the state of Connecticut). However, as the bill in the state legislature began to wend its way through the legislative process, the library directors of the public community colleges and the four Connecticut state universities began to see the handwriting on the wall.

The first meeting of the two groups occurred on March 18, 2011, when the community college library directors invited the CSU library directors to their monthly meeting. Also present at the meeting was the Connecticut state librarian, whose library was included in the shared library system used by the CSU libraries. At that first meeting the two groups broadly discussed joint interests: information literacy, off-site storage, and enhanced borrowing privileges for their respective students and faculty. The idea of a shared discovery tool to foster cross-institutional borrowing was also discussed. It was agreed that a future meeting would be desirable because the prospects for collaboration seemed promising, and the likelihood of consolidation of the two systems seemed imminent.

In September 2011, the chair of the Community Colleges Library Directors group reached out to the CSU library directors and invited them again to the October monthly meeting of the community colleges. A combined agenda was issued, and further discussion of potential shared initiatives led to the agreement between the two groups that a vision document should be prepared for the new Board of Regents. The two chairs of the respective library directors' groups worked closely on the draft and shared it with the full group for comment. This process further engaged the two groups, and the dialogue resulted in a document that was ready to send to the new Board of Regents as soon as they were officially named in January 2012. The areas of collaboration agreed upon were

- Information literacy
- Discovery platform: seamless interface to library resources
- Collaborative purchasing opportunities
- Shared off-site storage facility

The group also agreed on a name for their combined group: Council of Library Directors. To this point in less than a year, two groups that had never formally met together before had achieved a shared vision document and a new name. At the same time that this progress among the libraries was occurring, there was much going on in the surrounding political environment that reflected considerable concern about the merging of the two parent systems—community colleges and state universities—under one governing body. What were the factors that caused the libraries' directors to embrace collaboration and the individual institutions to be so wary of it?

Several primary factors motivated the library directors to support collaboration:

- There was a shared value system: all of the libraries agreed that it was all about the good of the students.
- There was a strong history among the libraries of loaning materials to each other as part of standard interlibrary loan procedures. Libraries cooperate and have a long history of cooperation.
- The collaboration was self-initiated; the Board of Regents had not even been formally appointed in 2011 when the libraries began their exploration of common goals.
- The library directors started to get to know each other better as they worked on the shared documents. The two chairs of the respective groups got along well.

Having created a shared vision and sent it to the Board of Regents, the Council of Library Directors decided to form task groups to begin to work together on the various initiatives. The directors agreed that a major priority would be to initiate a shared discovery platform. This project brought together various members of the staff of the two groups who developed specifications for an RFI (request for information) which was issued in 2012. The initial concept, to superimpose a single discovery system over the multiple legacy systems of the participating libraries, was eventually discarded in favor of seeking a single combined library system on the same platform. The rationale that led to this decision was that both legacy systems used by the CSCU libraries were becoming outdated, and one of the legacy systems had issued an end-of-support deadline of December 2016. Rather than invest substantial time and effort in integrating legacy systems via a shared discovery tool, it was ultimately determined to move forward with a new shared system.

Although it was agreed that a single shared system was the goal, it was not agreed which vendor's system of the two currently in use would be preferable. Both vendors were promoting their next-generation systems and both had a substantial market among academic libraries. A key question was whether an RFP (request for proposal) would be necessary (based on Connecticut state regulations) or whether the libraries could choose to migrate to one of the existing vendors' systems and upgrade to their next-generation system at the same time. Ultimately, the group decided that even if state regulations would permit a non-RFP process, it would be better to thoroughly examine the options in the current marketplace by issuing a formal RFP. An RFP Steering Committee was created led by two cochairs, each of whom was a library director, one from the community colleges and one from the universities. Six functional specification working groups were also established, with their representation and cochairs reflecting the community college and university constituencies. An aggressive time line was established and the process was greatly facilitated by having three staff from the IT (information technology) department at the Board of Regents assigned to the library project. One of these staff, a senior member of the IT organization, served as the project manager to facilitate communication and adherence to the time line. This connection to the Board of Regents' IT department fostered communication at the highest levels of the Board of Regents, whose budget was going to fund the project.

Much more could be said about this entire process, but I will focus on the leadership challenges.

The community colleges and the universities have different missions in that the former provide open access to higher education for a very wide array of students who may or may not be seeking a degree. The universities provide access to students who are ostensibly seeking a four-year degree and who must meet certain admission standards to enroll. The community colleges have a primary focus on teaching, whereas the universities have both a teaching and research expectation for their faculty. The colleges and universities under the Board of Regents range in size from small local campuses with modest collections and small library staffs to large PhD-granting institutions with large libraries, bigger budgets, and more specialized staff. The universities and the State Library had shared a single library system for over twenty years (Innovative Interfaces Inc. Millennium), whereas the community colleges have had individual independent instances of the same vendor's system (ExLibris Voyager) and never had to share system parameters.

With these disparities among the institutions and the libraries, several factors were key to promoting harmony and decision-making. The biggest two factors were a shared sense of mission in service to our collective 92,000 students, and trust in each other. It was clear that in a small state, students and adjunct faculty often enrolled in or taught classes at multiple campuses. Having a single library system would reduce the learning curve and make the combined resources easier to identify and share. Information literacy initiatives could be built on a single platform. Opportunities for mutually agreed-upon levels of shared collection development also could be provided in a single system.

Trust is something that can be elusive, but it has been critical to the success of the project to date. The library directors had been meeting approximately monthly since the Board of Regents was officially designated in 2012. The two cochairs of the council shared the duties of chairing the meetings and creating the agendas. They e-mailed each other and talked between meetings to make sure they were both on the same page. A variety of cooperative efforts (information literacy initiatives) created an early sense of shared purpose. A joint meeting of all available library staff of the seventeen libraries was held in July 2012 at one of the campuses and was facilitated by Marshall Breeding.

The various meetings, at which all voices were encouraged, gradually reinforced the sense of shared purpose and esprit de corps. Listening is also a big part of leadership. With such disparate libraries in the mix, there were naturally concerns that the bigger libraries might attempt to sway the discussions or the decisions in a way that would preempt the voices of the smaller libraries. While the discussions were frank and varying opinions were expressed, mutual respect was a key element in keeping the discussions civil and productively directed. During the months of discussion about how to proceed with the library system, there was a temptation to cut to the chase and go with one of the existing systems. This would have sped up the process, and provided a modicum of familiarity for some of the libraries, thereby easing the short-term pain of implementing a new system. However, past experience in another setting led this author to conclude that short-term gains were not worth long-term carping, and that a thorough if lengthy process would be worth the goodwill it was hoped it would generate. Going into the process, there was no assurance that consensus could be achieved. Each of the two groups tended to have a preference for the familiar vendor but no matter which one was chosen, there would be a learning curve.

Creating the Steering Committee structure and the functional working groups was extremely important in building consensus. So too was the arduous process of reviewing multiple RFP responses and hours of web-based demonstrations over the summer of 2015. The meetings of the functional working groups were time-intensive and really stretched the staff who had agreed to work on them. A sharing platform (base camp) which all interested staff could read and contribute to was also important in keeping the process open. The strong leadership of the two cochairs of the Steering Committee and their mutual goodwill were absolutely essential to moving the project forward.

At any point in this process, the forward momentum could have ground to a halt. And of course, not all was smooth. The aggressive time line led some committee members to withdraw and others had to pick up the slack. There were many comments on the base camp questioning assumptions, which led to follow-up questions with the bidding vendors. The answers were shared in a secure environment. All of this time-consuming and tedious process contributed to a sense that anyone who wanted to weigh in had an opportunity to do so.

As the August 2015 deadline for recommending the preferred vendor approached, there was a certain amount of anxiety over whether a consensus would be reached, or whether there would be a split decision leading to a potential impasse on the decision. A lot was at stake. However, in a secret ballot, the members of the Steering Committee unanimously recommended one vendor's system. In the meeting of the Council of Library Directors, who needed to approve the recommendation, the open vote was also unanimous.

It is clear that there will be many more leadership challenges in this project. Implementation will be fraught with numerous decisions big and small. There will be disagreements. But in the end, we hope that those two primary guiding principles of shared mission, and mutual trust and respect, will lead us forward to a new system that will benefit all of our students. It may not be a match made in heaven, but we believe it will be an amicable marriage of two library systems for the foreseeable future.

The following principles got us this far and will continue to guide us:

- Assume goodwill.
- Keep the dialogue open.
- Share your differences in a respectful manner.
- Don't try to coerce people to your point of view.
- Don't withdraw from the process when the going gets tough.
- Don't rush the process; buy-in takes time.
- Listen to all voices; people want to know that their point of view was fairly considered even if it didn't win the day.
- Don't make it personal; people may argue strongly for a particular issue or point of view, but it is not a personal affront.
- Thank people for their contributions to the shared project; inevitably some carry a larger share of the work than others, and their extra efforts should be acknowledged.
- Keep your eye on the goal.

- It is not about you; it is about the students.
- It is easy for groups to fracture around big decisions when so much is at stake; accept the decision and move on even if it didn't go your way.

NOTES

1. Central, Eastern, Southern, and Western Connecticut State Universities.
2. Asnuntuck, Capital, Gateway, Housatonic, Manchester, Middlesex, Naugatuck, Northwestern, Norwalk, Quinebaug, Three Rivers, and Tunxis Community Colleges.

EMY NELSON DECKER

4

The Sum of Its Parts

Building Teamwork in the Modern Academic Library Environment

THE MODERN ACADEMIC LIBRARY ENVIRONMENT requires a significant amount of collaboration with colleagues both inside the library and within the field at large. While graduate programs of study in library science often feature curricula that require a certain amount of "group work," specific instruction on how to be effective leading teams or how to encourage teamwork among one's associates is often lacking. This leaves only specialized leadership training courses or traditional on-the-job experience as the main venues for the library leader to learn about team building. The ability to build teamwork, however, is a skill set that can and should be developed because it is crucial to implementing all aspects of the organization's strategic plan down to ensuring the functionality of essential day-to-day library operations. In this chapter, I will consider team building through specific topics: communication styles, generational differences, and strategies for targeting the unique strengths of individuals toward the common goals of the library. The discussion that follows is from my own experience in building a team, and the lessons I have learned in so doing.

COMMUNICATION STYLES

While effective communication is key to any human relationship, it is particularly essential when building a team and encouraging participation from team members toward a library goal. Of course, communication styles vary significantly from person to person, and while a proactive leader will focus on communicating as clearly and consistently with her direct reports as possible, there are subtleties of communication that often have to be learned—and then nuanced—on the job.

Technologies like e-mail are vital to communication in today's academic environment, but people consider e-mail differently. For me, e-mail is a way of communicating information that is useful but not necessarily urgent. I appreciate e-mail because it allows me to type out my thoughts, reread the e-mail for clarity, and then send it to my direct reports for their later consumption. In other words, my message will be waiting for them when they check their e-mail at some point during the day. When I communicate via e-mail, I'm sending information that my direct reports will need in order to accomplish their assignments and I am providing a virtual paper trail of the information. I am also signaling to them that the contents of the message are worth reading and absorbing, but are not time-sensitive or overly pressing.

Not all of my direct reports are such fans of e-mail. In fact, some of them find e-mail to be cold or distant, off-putting, or even annoying. For those who do not like e-mail, receiving multiple messages each day can be grating and can cause them to disengage, which is hardly the desired outcome. This can be exacerbated if other members of the team respond to those e-mails, filling in-boxes with still more messages. I learned this lesson about e-mail when a direct report of mine acted somewhat removed from a project that I had been discussing primarily by e-mail. I referenced the e-mail thread and was informed that he found the number of e-mails I sent difficult to keep up with, and he also felt that it was hard to follow the content of them. This surprised me, because I had thought that sending e-mail would promote both retention of directions and engagement with the initiative as it developed. Understanding his dislike of e-mail made me reconsider my heavy use of it. I reasoned that if most of the team's communications were taking place via e-mail and he was struggling to engage in this way, he would eventually become separated from the team. Realizing the seriousness of this potential outcome, I made an effort to limit my number of e-mail communications per day and to save discussions about project directions and collaborative opportunities for weekly team meetings.

In addition to adjusting my personal communication style as part of team building, I also learned how to foster intra-team communication to promote team solidarity. During weekly team meetings, I made it a constant agenda item that one person would contribute a brief overview of the main takeaways they had gotten from a recent conference, workshop, event, or webinar to share with the team. Since each of my direct reports knew that they would be responsible for this activity, they began focusing their skills in summarizing the main points of a presentation and in articulating how the information they had recently acquired could best benefit their teammates. These weekly meetings, while informal and taking place among team members who knew each other well, helped to develop my direct reports' confidence in speaking and presenting.

Many professionals in the academic library sphere could benefit from honing their presentation skills, and my starting this weekly practice arena gave them this opportunity. I recommend an informal setting to encourage direct reports to learn how to present and communicate effectively. A debriefing session following a collaborative project is another method of opening communication that will give direct reports an opportunity to reflect on the activity and suggest strategies to improve in the future (Eddy, Tannenbaum, and Mathieu, 2013). Again, a friendly setting, with open feedback and supportive colleagues, will aid in maximizing this opportunity for self-improvement and enhanced team camaraderie.

GENERATIONAL DIFFERENCES

The current academic environment includes members from several different generations. I have supervised a range of age groups ranging from young professionals in their first jobs to professionals who are in the twilight of their careers. There is plenty of literature describing the specific differences between Millennials and Baby Boomers, but nothing written truly prepares a leader for supervising the members of these vastly different generations. As a member of Gen X, I am situated, chronologically, between the Millennials and the Baby Boomers that I supervise. No longer being the youngest in the workforce and not yet the eldest provides me with a unique perspective.

While the goal of a leader is to treat all direct reports equally, knowing how to reach them comes with a learning curve. I presently have a member representing each generation—Millennials, Gen X, and Baby Boomers—as direct reports. I was warned that members of the Baby Boom generation might challenge my authority, but that warning was mired in generational stereotyping, as I have not come across this even once in my setting. I try to remain mindful of generational trends when leading my team members, but some of their needs relate more to individual personalities than to true generational differences, of course. That said, some key differences between the generations emerge:

- Baby Boomers, for the most part, value hard work and respect; they particularly expect the respect of their younger colleagues.
- Gen Xers tend to be annoyed by bureaucratic "red tape"; they like to work in a flexible environment that allows them to solve problems in the way they see fit.
- Millennials are interested in getting to participate and contribute to a larger goal and want to be recognized for their efforts.

In order to build a team that works well together with members from each of these different generations, I work to develop projects, or facets of projects, that will appeal to each generation. For example, asking a member of the Baby Boomer generation to give his input on an issue can go a long way toward showing respect for his knowledge and experience. I supervise someone who is a member of the Baby Boomer generation who has also spent his entire career at this particular library. His vast institutional memory makes it easy to recognize his expertise by asking him to explain to me and the rest of the team how an event or project may have taken place at the library in previous years. I also ask him to provide critical feedback on how we can improve upon the previous method of completing the project.

My direct report who is a member of Generation X becomes annoyed when she feels stymied by what she views as too many layers of approval. I find that when I ask her to explain why she thinks the "checks and balances" are in place, she relaxes into a better headspace and it reenergizes her to pursue another avenue for completing a project or working within the existing administrative parameters. Exploring other options for bringing a project to fruition also allows her to work in a flexible and creative way that she enjoys. As a member of Generation X, myself, I often identify closely with her frustration, but in my role as a leader I require her to look past the initial annoyance, explain it out loud so that she is in touch with the "why" aspect of any given policy, and we move along from there. Unlike the Baby Boomers and Gen Xers who tend to prefer specific recognition for a job well done and like to be rewarded for it, my Millennial direct report much prefers to be thanked for her contribution to a project. She seems to eschew taking direct leadership or ownership of a task but instead takes a lot of pride in researching, discovering, and employing an overall collaborative approach, and when she can turn the results of these actions into a deliverable, she reports feeling the most edified.

It is important, however, to realize that as is true with any grouping of human beings, generational trends do not always correspond to the individual. As Mayah and Gedro (2014) suggest, age should be considered in relation to other factors such as race, gender, and so on. While it is useful to understand the hallmarks of generations, ascribing everything that tends to be true of a generation to one person whose birth year falls within those parameters can be as dangerous as any other type of stereotyping (Barnes, 2013). Individuals, particularly direct reports, should be valued and understood for their unique strengths. A forward-thinking leader will also identify their specific weaknesses and then target these as areas for skills development opportunities.

TARGETING THE UNIQUE
STRENGTHS OF INDIVIDUALS

Generally speaking, people tend to enjoy doing what they are good at doing. It is worthwhile to ask employees what they enjoy and what they envision as being their ideal career path (Freeman, 2013). When I build a team, I work to identify both the strengths and interests of my direct reports in order to customize projects, whenever possible, to them. For example, I have one direct report who enjoys creating soundtracks and movies and is well-versed in using audiovisual editing software. I have asked her to develop instruction videos covering the use of library services and to make other videos for online courses, student orientations, and teaching aids to assist library instruction. Since working in the library's audiovisual studio is something she enjoys, she can incorporate her hobby into her work and produce excellent learning aids for the benefit of her team, her colleagues, and our library users. Another direct report of mine is a self-proclaimed "techie" and she researches new and emerging technologies for personal enjoyment, so I have turned this into a professional task for her, too. I have her submit a report to me on a quarterly basis about new applications, software, or hardware that she has researched with an explanation of how the library could benefit from adopting this technology. While the budget ultimately has to be taken into consideration, having her contribute her ideas of the best technology for the library keeps her engaged and contributing to the library's goal of using the best of today's technology for our faculty, students, and staff.

I have learned that asking people to contribute something that they enjoy and that they feel utilizes their hard-won skills causes them to engage with the project and to feel good about their contribution to the greater goal. Work feels less like work when you are able to do something you enjoy and you are praised for your execution of the task. Early on in my career as a library leader, I wish I had known how to target the unique strengths of individuals to get the best results. When I started out, I labored under the impression that it was necessary to ensure that all team members developed roughly similar skill sets in any of the required tasks of the job. I now understand the power of letting individuals shine at what they are best at doing.

However, it is impossible to be good at doing everything, and there are some critical skill sets that must be developed. In order to promote my direct reports' active participation in the day-to-day work of the library, I set up mini-workshops wherein the team member with the skill teaches the other team members who need to learn the skill. I select at least one topic that each team member can teach to the others. These workshops, like the mini-reports made during weekly meetings, promote confidence, instruction, and presentation skills. They are also a great way to cross-train direct reports and showcase the special skills of each team member.

TEAM BUILDING FOR LIBRARY LEADERS

It is an unfortunate reality that leaders of the modern academic library often receive little or no training in the art of team building prior to their taking leadership. A key component of leadership is the ability to unite people and foster an environment wherein individuals wish to contribute their skills for the good of the team and for the success of the library. While I have redoubled my efforts to acquire team-building leadership training by attending sessions at professional conferences that center on team building and by attending leadership institutes, I was already acting in a leadership role prior to my completing these trainings. This is the case for many library leaders. During my journey, I experimented with different methods for promoting team engagement and camaraderie and have found several strategies that deliver pleasing results. When it comes to team building, I have found that the method of communication can be just as important as the message. If a leader is not communicating with direct reports in a format that resonates with them, the message may be lost or, worse, the team may begin to become resentful and disengaged.

It is also important to realize that the contemporary working environment represents members of the Baby Boom generation, Gen Xers, and, increasingly, Millennials. The background and context for each generation is worth understanding, but a leader must be careful not to go so far overboard with generational thinking as to reduce individuals to generational stereotypes. Another strategy for building a team centers on allowing direct reports to shine by incorporating activities that allow them to demonstrate their skills, talents, and interests. A team that works well together, values each other's contributions, and is committed to not only the successful completion of a project but to reaching and exceeding library goals likely has an effective and forward-thinking leader at the helm. The goal of a library leader should be the cultivation of a highly functioning team that sees both their roles and their successful contributions toward library objectives.

REFERENCES

Barnes, A. Keith. 2013. "Breaking through Generational Stereotypes." *T+D* 67, no. 6: 30–33.

Eddy, Erik R., Scott I. Tannenbaum, and John E. Mathieu. 2013. "Helping Teams to Help Themselves: Comparing Two Team-Led Debriefing Methods." *Personnel Psychology* 66, no. 4: 975–1008.

Freeman, Caryn. 2013. "Making Sure Employees Are Engaged Should Be Employer Priority." *HR Focus* 90, no. 10: 8.

Mayah, Angela Titi, and Julie Gedro. 2014. "Understanding Generational Diversity: Strategic Human Resource Management and Development across the Generational 'Divide.'" *New Horizons in Adult Education & Human Resource Development* 26, no. 2: 36–48.

BRADFORD LEE EDEN

5

Iterative Strategic Planning

Lessons Learned in the Trenches

STRATEGIC PLANNING: for many, these two words evoke visions of long, regularly scheduled weekly meetings for months on end; endless discussions and constant battles over wording, representation, and priorities; and in the end a long document that everyone looks at once or twice, puts in an online folder or places on their library website, and then immediately forgets about it in exhaustion or frustration. And this is just the internal, library process; trying to gain participation in the broader, university-related process of institutional strategic planning is another challenge. If the library is lucky enough to gain representation, then there is an educational and positioning challenge regarding what exactly the library is and what it does, and how it can contribute to and enhance the university's objectives, goals, and action items. In the end, there then needs to be a realignment and readjustment of the library's strategic plan with that of the parent institution, in order to indicate the library's collaborative and partnering relationship within the broader institutional priorities. A convoluted process, to say the least!

A better strategy, if it is possible, is for the library to align itself directly with the strategic planning time line of the university itself. Unfortunately, most universities work on a five- to ten-year strategic plan, namely because of the magnification of the challenges mentioned above, although the current higher education landscape is now requiring colleges and universities to reexamine, intensify, and market their objectives and priorities on a more regular basis. The best strategy is to have an iterative strategic plan, given the incredible pace of technological and political developments. This iterative process needs to be transparent and inclusive of everyone in the organization; it needs to be unobtrusive and painless given the limited amount of time that people can adequately devote to the process; and it requires a certain amount of experimentation and negotiation between and among everyone in the organization. This chapter will provide a quick description of the iterative strategic planning process within the Christopher Center Library at Valparaiso University (Indiana), some historical background on the author's experiences, and some quick tips for success.

BACKGROUND

The author has been involved in strategic planning at three institutions: the University of Nevada, Las Vegas (UNLV) (two times); the University of California, Santa Barbara (UCSB) (two times); and Valparaiso University (VU) (five times). Each time was a learning experience, given that two of these schools were large research universities, while the author's current position is at a medium-sized private university. The first time strategic planning was attempted at UNLV was in the early 2000s, after moving into a brand-new, $58,000,000 state-of-the-art library. Because there were many internal constituencies and departments that wanted to be involved in the process, the planning committee was huge: well over twenty people. One can imagine the complexity of trying to plan a series of meetings which twenty people are able to attend on a regular basis. As department heads in a fairly competitive and fiefdom-like environment, the meetings were highly charged and discussions were largely related to power and political motivations. The process took over a year to finish, and when it was done, everyone was so exhausted that the strategic plan was shared, posted online, and basically forgotten. The goals and directions were basically words on a piece of paper; no one person or department was invested in the document as a whole, and no measurable or actionable items were assigned to anyone or any department as a responsibility line. In the end, this first exercise in strategic planning was very frustrating and many felt it was a waste of time, although representation and overall organizational participation seemed to be the main purpose of the exercise. The UNLV Libraries attempted one more strategic plan in the mid-2000s before the author moved on to UCSB; this second exercise at UNLV comprised a much smaller committee, with more open meetings for organizational participation and inclusion; in the end, the information learned from the first process assisted in less overall investment of time and effort, but still no responsibility lines or deadlines for meeting goals.

The University of California, Santa Barbara, as an Association of Research Libraries member and Research 1 university, was and is part of the largest academic library consortium in the world: the University of California (UC). There were a number of challenges related to strategic planning for UCSB during the five years the author was there: no leadership (the university librarian position was open for three of the five years, with a commuter university librarian for a short time who was not really invested in the library or institution); the Great Recession of 2009 (which deflected the university system from any long-term strategic planning, and made California the poster child of the recession); and a chancellor who spoke highly of the library but never provided an increase in the library's budget. Because of these challenges, the associate university librarians (AULs) acted as a team for most of the author's tenure there, working together on strategic initiatives such as a new library building addition that was finally moved to priority status by the state; development and fund-raising activities; and systemwide Next Generation Technical Services (NGTS) task forces that tried to negotiate innovative strategies for collaborative library partnerships in order to reduce library costs and save money. The two strategic exercises attempted during this time period were much more reserved, given the budget situation of UCSB as well as the UC system. Again, organizational involvement was crucial, and the AULs worked hard to present a united front regarding directions and priorities at a time when few resources were available. There was much more success with strategic planning at UCSB because goals were assigned responsibility lines, which meant that someone was assigned to make sure that the goal was getting done or accomplished.

CURRENT SITUATION

As the incoming dean of library services at the Christopher Center for Library and Information Resources (CCLIR) at Valparaiso University in 2011, I was surprised to find a university organization that was based on iterative strategic planning. Valparaiso University is a medium-sized, private, independent Lutheran university which had hired a new president in 2008 who understood the importance of constantly providing direction and aspirations for the university. This was also due in part to an engaged Board of Directors which wanted to see clear objectives, goals, and action items for moving the university forward. As a result, and wishing to emulate the university's strategic planning in the library, the author centered CCLIR's strategic planning process around that of VU (November through October), and each year has provided an opportunity to try a different approach to the process as well as learn what works and doesn't work within the current library organization.

In 2011, when I first started in the dean of library services position, the major area of concern and need from both library faculty and staff was copyright issues related to author rights, a new institutional repository (Bepress/ Digital Commons), scholarly communication, and open access. In addition, both internal and external communication challenges prompted me to implement a top-down approach to strategic planning during my first year. This worked quite well, given that I was new and entering the situation with a fresh perspective and mind-set, and it meant that library faculty and staff could comment on a draft mission, vision, and goals statement and plan with action items without a large investment of time. Alignment with the university strategic plan was not the first consideration, given the number of challenges and needs within the library in the areas of copyright training, communication, marketing, information literacy, and assessment. Various task forces were set up to focus on these areas, many of which have since morphed into standing committees.

Once I was involved in the university's iterative strategic planning cycle (May through November), the library faculty and staff were very interested in a more direct and inclusive approach to the library's strategic planning process. In 2013, therefore, I tried a bottom-up approach to strategic planning, where a blank whiteboard was set up and voluntary meetings were held to discuss each of the university's goals, how they aligned with the library, and what objectives and action items were appropriate for the coming year. This method proved to be culture-driven, and was quite successful in that everyone who participated got to discuss and be involved in the draft process. While more time was invested by everyone in this approach, it produced a much more meaningful and organizationally driven strategic plan that resulted in a greater investment of morale and negotiation in the end product. I also put together a responsibilities document that linked one person in the library as the key leader/reporter on each action item in the strategic plan; this helped to set up accountability and make the strategic plan something living within the organization. A midyear report to everyone on the status of action items was also instituted, thus helping to keep the strategic plan moving forward as well as remind everyone of what needed to be accomplished before the end of the strategic planning cycle.

At the same time as the 2013–14 library strategic plan was at the midyear report, the university was beginning its next phase of strategic planning for the 2014–15 cycle. For me, this became an opportunity to align the library's strategic planning cycle with that of the university. Discussions began in the library prior to the May deans and directors' strategic planning retreat, for library faculty and staff to assist me with inserting key library-related objectives and action items into the university's strategic plan, for when I attended the retreat. This process helped to guide me in the high-level university drafts of the strategic plan that took place at this retreat, knowing that the objectives were from the organization rather than from me alone. It also provided an opportunity for me to bring back, early in the library's strategic planning process, what high-level activities and plans the university was hoping to move forward on in the coming year, thus helping the library to plan and align its strategic plan accordingly. In addition to this overall structure, I tried to mix up the library's strategic planning process by starting with the previous year's plan as a basis to build the new strategic plan (neither top-down or bottom-up, but a combination of both). This approach had mixed results: while overall participation time was much less of an investment than the bottom-up method, it also meant that the organizational culture was not as grounded in the strategic plan that eventually emerged. While everyone in the library was on board with the new strategic plan, some felt that it wasn't as open or negotiated as much as the previous year's plan.

Moving into the most recent strategic planning cycle (2015–16), I decided to try another approach: that of directed conversations for each goal in both the university's and the library's strategic plans, led by two members of the library faculty/staff. Given that there are currently five goals, this meant that ten library faculty/staff would be leading the development of the objectives and goals rather than me alone. This was another type of mixed approach, more bottom-up than top-down, and it also provided opportunities for others within the organization to lead and direct the strategic planning process. There was much more discussion and development at this preliminary stage, which then moved into a high-level meeting of everyone within the organization to reflect on the process and bring the document together into a final form as a group. The process of graying-out action items for future consideration was incorporated (which is used in the university's process), and this also helped the library to think in the long term about action items beyond the current year's resources (both people and finances). As always, once the strategic plan was finalized, a responsibilities document was also produced, and the library's new strategic plan for the year was placed on the library's website (http://library.valpo.edu/mission.html).

CONCLUSION

To develop successful strategies, an organization must simultaneously carefully plan and act upon opportunities, have a broad vision and focus on details, and establish direction from the top but also embrace participation from all levels within the organization (Matthews, 2005, 7). This chapter provides a brief description of one person's experiences of directing and leading strategic planning throughout his career. One thing that I have learned (the hard way) is that there is no right or wrong way to do strategic planning. Yes, there are strategies, schools of thought, and types (see Matthews, 2005 for an overview), and there are processes and tools. Can I say that I have always done it right? Definitely not. Can I say that I have tried to work within the overall local organizational culture and mood to experiment with different approaches for strategic planning? Yes. In my experience, library strategic planning can and should be an iterative process, given the pace of change within libraries and higher education. It should be as unobtrusive as possible, so that it doesn't interrupt or inhibit current operations, given that we are all understaffed and still need to get the daily work of the library done. It should be as inclusive and open as possible, centered around the discussion and negotiation of current challenges, opportunities, and directions by both the library and the parent institution. It should be linked, guided, and even mirror if possible the university's mission, vision, goals, objectives, and action items. Finally, in order to be successful, it needs to have actionable and measurable goals and action items, with stated responsibility lines. A midyear update to the organization on the status of current action items is crucial for success as well. In the end, a mix of project management, a lot of empathy and listening time, and a sprinkle of writing skills need to be added to bring the document to completion. As I have found, practice doesn't necessarily make perfect, but it certainly helps in the learning process.

RECOMMENDED READING

Gaspar, Deborah B. 2015. "Strategic Vision: Navigating Change." *College & Research Libraries News* 76, no. 7: 380–83.

Giesecke, Joan, Jon Cawthorne, and Deb Pearson. 2015. *Navigating the Future with Scenario Planning: A Guidebook for Librarians.* Chicago: Association of College and Research Libraries.

Matthews, Joseph R. 2005. *Strategic Planning and Management for Library Managers.* Westport, CT: Libraries Unlimited.

6

So, You Find Yourself
Supervising Faculty Librarians

What Now?

ABOUT HALF OF ACADEMIC LIBRARIANS in the United States have
faculty status, though the specifics of this status vary by institution (Bolin,
2008). In my career as a librarian since 1992 I have held faculty status at four
institutions: two public universities and two private liberal arts colleges. I am
agnostic when it comes to the value of faculty status for academic librarians,
the libraries we administer, and the institutions we serve. Faculty status can
be either a help or a hindrance in providing library services, depending on the
institutional context, the specifics of such status, and the faculty and administrative cultures. I disagree with the idea that faculty status for librarians is
a marker of respect and is necessary for us to be regarded as equal and valued
partners by other faculty members. All other things being equal, the value
we contribute as librarians is independent of our employment status. Value is
defined by what we do, not our status. However, all other things are not always
equal. There are stratified institutions at which faculty members interact with
each other in ways different from those in which they interact with staff
or administrators. Even at these institutions, formal faculty status may not

gain librarians entry into the faculty community. The status of librarians should meet the long-term needs and support the mission of the institution. The library and the librarians need sufficient autonomy and professional control to be able to effectively serve the needs of the institution. Faculty status may be an appropriate way of ensuring such autonomy and control.

ON BECOMING A DIRECTOR

A new director leading a group of faculty librarians should begin thinking about the issues involved before assuming the position of director. While the employment status of the librarians will not be the most important aspect of a directorship, it is important to understand the employment status of all individuals in the organization before accepting a position in order to incorporate this into a holistic understanding of the library.

As I do in the introduction, you should be able to articulate your own position with regard to faculty status for librarians. When searching for or considering positions, seek information about the status of the position and that of the librarians with whom you might be working. As the search proceeds, gather more specifics. The specifics of eligibility and criteria for tenure, the system of ranks and promotion, the librarians' roles within faculty governance, and within the governance of the library, will all vary. This is also true of the status of the director's position. Details matter, and these details will not always be clear in job ads, position descriptions, or accessible websites or documents. Pick the appropriate moment in the search process to ask for this information, and when you are in a position to hire faculty librarians, make sure that the details of faculty status are explicitly outlined in writing and shared at the appropriate stage. The more you know going in, the better chance you, and the librarians you supervise, have of being successful and happy.

THE DIRECTOR'S ROLES

The employment status of the library director also varies. In larger universities the director may be a dean of a school consisting of the library system and the librarians within it. In smaller institutions the director may be a department chair. In one small liberal arts college, the director's role is elected from among the tenured librarians and rotates periodically. In my case, depending on the circumstances, I act as an administrator managing a complex organization, a faculty department chair facilitating the work of a group of faculty colleagues, and a dean reporting to the provost. Try to understand how others see you, both within and beyond the library. Are you an administrator with faculty status or a faculty member who performs administrative duties? Also recognize that the answer to this question is context-sensitive and that how you understand and perform your role has a great deal of influence upon how others see you.

The status of the library director also influences your relationship with faculty librarians. Be explicit with your colleagues about the nature of your role and try to understand their expectations of you. Hopefully, this will be explicitly stated in written documents like the faculty handbook or procedural manuals. If it is not, you can encourage this to be rectified. Even if not explicitly stated, take a moment to make sure everyone is clear about your role in a particular circumstance (a tenure review, a hiring process, or a planning process). In the circumstances at hand, are you one colleague among many, or a dean with a separate and different role, or something in between? Be consistent; you damage your credibility if you agree to act as one among equals and then veto a decision made by the majority.

HIRING, REVIEWING, AND MANAGING FACULTY LIBRARIANS

The employment status of librarians as faculty members will have an impact on the hiring process, the applicants attracted to the position, and the attributes you seek in a successful candidate. Often the hiring process for faculty members is defined in the faculty bylaws or the faculty handbook. Understand these rules, how they have been practiced in previous library hires, and how much variation is tolerated in this library and in the wider campus faculty culture.

In any hiring process, the goal is to attract the best candidate possible to fulfill the responsibilities of the position and further the mission of the institution. It is unethical, for instance, to hire a tenure-track librarian if you do not think she can succeed in achieving tenure. It is also inefficient, since tenure-track positions are generally "up or out": achieve tenure or leave, and the library may have to repeat the hiring process within six years, or even lose the position. The research and publication requirements for tenure vary enormously, but they can be a stumbling block for some librarians. It is important to be explicit about these requirements early in the hiring process and to incorporate ways of evaluating applicants' potential in this regard. Do applicants have prior research, publication, or professional presentation experience? What methodological preparation do they have? How engaged are they with a research literature (perhaps, but not necessarily, library science), and can they write or speak intelligently about their potential research interests? Similar questions can be asked about teaching, which is perhaps the most common element of faculty status. Incorporating such questions into the hiring process can reveal, to both parties, the candidate's potential to thrive or not as both a librarian and a faculty member.

Since there is little or no prejudice against faculty librarians moving in mid-career (as there is in many other academic fields), you may seek or attract mid-career professionals. These candidates can raise specific questions. Is your faculty salary structure flexible enough to accommodate candidates who may seek higher salaries than a candidate with a freshly minted PhD? Does a record of publication and service at other institutions count for anything in your promotion and tenure system? If candidates come from institutions with faculty status, how does your institution handle requests to retain rank and tenure? Just as you will have to find an appropriate place within a community of faculty librarians, as director you have a responsibility to help more experienced newly hired faculty librarians find their place as well.

A director's role in helping to support librarians meet the criteria set for faculty does not end at hiring. Find out how the library has supported faculty librarians in the past. Is there a formal or informal mentoring program in place? Is there a system to evaluate progress towards tenure or promotion (if applicable)? If faculty librarians are expected to teach, to publish or present, to be active in professional organizations, or to participate in faculty governance, are there clear expectations about how to balance the time for such activities with their specific responsibilities as librarians? Are adequate funds available to support faculty librarian travel and publication expenses? Some answers will be library-specific, but it is also important to understand whether faculty librarians have access to the funding and opportunities open to all faculty members. Like all faculty, librarians can struggle to find adequate time to pursue all three legs of the faculty stool—teaching (or librarianship), research, and service. The best advice I ever received in this regard is to find the sweet spot where all three overlap so that your research and service inform your librarianship and vice versa.

At Rollins College (Florida) we decided that we also needed to find a way to put the joy back into research, writing, and publication, and keep our focus on our research. As director, I took on the task of convening what we call the Research and Publication Group. All untenured faculty librarians are invited to join the group, which meets once a month for just one hour. A librarian takes the lead each time we meet, perhaps describing an idea for research, circulating a draft before the meeting for comment and discussion, or asking for ideas on a suitable publishing outlet for a manuscript. We also go around the table and update each other on progress in our scholarship. We celebrate successful publications, we commiserate over rejected manuscripts or research that did not pan out, and we discuss how to respond to calls for revisions. Most importantly, we do so in a supportive and nonjudgmental way, as a group of colleagues all striving to produce the best scholarship we can. Over the years we have developed a range and depth of experience in research methods, book and journal editing, and manuscript review. Everyone at the table is able to take advantage of the collective wisdom of the group.

If faculty status for librarians is important to the library's success in advancing the mission of the institution, then the expenses (both time and money) involved in enabling librarians to succeed as faculty members must be factored in to the cost of library services. However, there are two parties that gain from successful faculty librarians: the library and the wider institution, and the individual librarian in terms of continued career growth beyond the institution. Therefore, it is not necessary to budget for 100 percent of the money and time expended in these activities. Model faculty members spend funds from external grants, their institution's funds, and their own time and money on research, travel, and professional engagement. They spend long hours in the lab, the archive, and the field. They write on weekends and in the evening. They do this because this work brings not only prestige and rewards to their institution, but pleasure to themselves as well. Faculty librarians should also expect to follow this model. This is a professional vocation, not just a job.

A new director leading a library and group of faculty librarians will find librarians at all stages of their careers—tenure track, relatively new librarians, as well as tenured librarians, including senior faculty members. Achieving the markers of faculty status are not hoops to be jumped through, after which the faculty member falls gently back to earth and enjoys an unproductive life of leisure and guaranteed employment. The granting of tenure and promotion comes with an expectation of continued professional growth and productivity. A faculty librarian should be at least as, if not more, productive as a scholar, and more expert as a teacher and librarian, after tenure than before. It is too common for librarians to see faculty promotion and tenure requirements as external to their librarianship and to seek to meet those requirements in order to pursue their true passion, librarianship. If faculty status is an important element in successfully serving your institution, then these requirements are integral parts of being a faculty librarian. As a new director you can help your librarian colleagues understand their faculty status as part of their librarianship. More senior faculty librarians can also be key mentors in helping their colleagues grow into their role in the professoriate.

Promotion to full professor should come with the expectation of expertise and leadership on campus and beyond. Unless a new director has been able to negotiate tenure and a senior rank upon hiring, he or she may be outranked by these librarians. Approach the presence of such senior faculty leadership in the library as a blessing. You have inherited years, perhaps decades of experience, deep expertise, and an opportunity for collaborative leadership.

Sometimes, however, senior faculty librarians can be negative forces in the library. They may not have kept their skills up to date, they may be wedded to outdated practices, or they may seek to exert undue influence over their untenured colleagues. This can happen in any library, but faculty status and particularly tenure can leave a new director with the impression that senior tenured librarians are untouchable. Nothing could be further from the truth. As director you are charged with the administration of the library and the deployment of resources, including the human resources, to meet the community's information needs. If a tenured librarian is unable or unwilling to enact the mission and plan of the library, a new director would be remiss in allowing this to continue.

Hopefully the library's plan is developed in collaboration with the faculty librarians, and any disagreements or professional development and retraining needs are resolved during the planning process. But if this situation continues, make sure the senior administrator to whom you report is fully aware of the situation and supports your intention to resolve it. Try to develop with the librarian in question a mutually acceptable plan for improvement. If the librarian's inability or unwillingness to perform continues, investigate your institutional faculty policies with regard to tenured-faculty performance. Ultimately, if necessary, look to the procedures outlined in the AAUP's 1958 "Statement on Procedural Standards in Faculty Dismissal Proceedings" (American Association of University Professors, 1958). Throughout the process, make sure you have the full support of your administration and your human resources department; make sure that you follow all institutional procedures; and make sure that you are truly working in the best interest of the library and the community you serve and have not become embroiled in a personal vendetta against an obstinate colleague.

The divide between faculty and staff that is so common in higher education may manifest itself in a library, which tends to have a greater proportion of nonfaculty staff members than other departments in which faculty reside. This divide can be exacerbated in merged IT/library organizations and as libraries increasingly hire what James Neal referred to as "feral librarians" (Neal, 2006). As a new director, you can either ameliorate or aggravate this divide. If you have read this far, you should be clear about why faculty status is important, or not, in your library and you should know that faculty status comes with responsibilities as well as rights. Find ways to help everyone in the library understand this. Celebrate faculty publication and professional leadership successes and the hard, but often hidden, work that goes into making those possible. Consider requiring a report at all staff meetings from faculty librarians returning from conferences and sabbaticals, and conversely find ways to show how much you value the contributions of staff without faculty status. But don't expect to entirely overcome this divide, because it is a perennial issue in higher education.

BEYOND THE LIBRARY

Within institutional parameters, the faculty as a body determine their own criteria for success, promotion, and tenure. Individual faculty members have wide latitude in organizing their work to meet those criteria. Within the core faculty in academic departments this autonomy and self-governance works well, but the expectations of the library can be at odds with the expectations of the faculty. At the level of the individual faculty librarian, this can come down to expectations for promotion and tenure that are at odds with the administrative expectations of library managers and the administrators to whom the library reports. In such cases, what is a librarian to do? Achieve tenure and disappoint their supervisor, or meet the expectations of their supervisor and lose their job because they failed to achieve tenure? What is a director to do in such circumstances?

First, understand that faculty expectations, especially around promotion and tenure, change very slowly, tend to be conservative, and are jealously protected. If there is a faculty union and a contract involved, change can be even more difficult to achieve. Expectations can change, but this will take time and is likely to be more successful if the impetus comes from within the faculty. Work with your faculty, especially your senior faculty librarians, to bring both sets of expectations into alignment. But do so after you have explored all other possibilities, which might include reconceptualizing administrative responsibilities to better fit with faculty expectations, and educating non-librarian faculty involved in faculty reviews about librarianship.

Even more important is helping faculty librarians understand faculty culture and modeling "facultiness" for them. One of the by-products of doctoral programs is the acculturation of a new generation of scholars into the faculty. This acculturation is reinforced in postdoctorate fellowships and in first faculty positions. The MLS degree does not do this. So one of the reasons why some librarians with faculty status are not regarded as "real" faculty by their colleagues outside the library is that we think and act differently. If nonlibrarian faculty think about the dean or department chair at all, it is as a senior colleague or someone whose job it is to arrange the resources for the faculty member to succeed in teaching and research. Often a faculty member's first loyalty is to his discipline. The college or university is simply an institutional arrangement that enables (or thwarts) his passion for scholarship, teaching, and status within his discipline.

Librarians tend to have a more corporate or administrative relationship with their department head and institution. As a new director, consider hiring librarians who enjoy spending time with other faculty members, the intellectual life of the faculty, and the cut and thrust of faculty culture. Look for ways to expose librarians to this culture. Are they invited to and are attending convocations and other ceremonies? Are librarians attending faculty presentations and lectures on campus? Are they intellectually engaged in their own sub-discipline of librarianship (reading the literature, participating in conferences, etc.), and is your library providing opportunities to discuss new developments in librarianship, not just with an eye to immediate application in your service to users, but on a more theoretical level? Model faculty are intellectually engaged; faculty librarians should be too. Just as importantly, as a new director, are you modeling such behaviors?

Not infrequently the idea that librarians are not "real" faculty and should not have faculty status extends to the administration of the institution. This lack of administrative support can stem from beliefs about the nature of the faculty and the nature of librarianship, but it can also stem from a desire to have more flexibility with regard to employment. This might not mean that your provost plans to fire librarians, but that budgetary policies make faculty lines more expensive than staff, or they hear that libraries are changing and librarians are re-skilling, and they are trying to retain long-term institutional flexibility. It is possible that you will find an administration that seeks to reclassify librarians from staff to faculty status. If you are clear on why you think that faculty status is, or is not, important for librarians at your institution, you are well positioned to either work with your administration to change the employment status of librarians, or to defend the current status. This question can arise when a new president, provost, or dean is appointed. So keep your political antennae active and always be aware of the shifting political landscape within which you work.

CONCLUSION

Over my career as a faculty librarian, a supervisor of faculty librarians, and eventually a director, I have come to realize that there are three things that are most significant in dealing with an issue like faculty status for librarians. First, know thyself; understand your own position vis-à-vis faculty status, reflect on this occasionally, and test it against differing positions in the literature and among your colleagues. The better you understand your own position, the better able you will be to support the faculty librarians with whom you work and to challenge them to meet the high expectations that come with faculty status. Second, understand the structural setting of policies, procedures, and decision-making bodies that frame faculty status in your library and institution, and the ever-changing political landscape that supports or challenges faculty status for librarians. But also understand that neither is set in stone. Finally, understand the environment in which you work. If faculty status is an important part of how you best serve your community, model the best faculty behavior for the librarians with whom you work and expect the highest standards of librarianship, teaching, scholarship, and service from them and yourself. No one ever said being a new director was going to be easy, but it will be rewarding.

REFERENCES

American Association of University Professors. 1958. "Statement on Procedural Standards in Faculty Dismissal Proceedings." www.aaup.org/report/statement-procedural-standards-faculty-dismissal-proceedings.

Bolin, M. K. 2008. "A Typology of Librarian Status at Land Grant Universities." *The Journal of Academic Librarianship* 34, no. 3: 220–30.

Neal, James G. 2006. "Raised by Wolves." *Library Journal*, February 15, 42–44.

KIM CLARKE

7

It's Always Personal

Developing an Awareness
of Employment Law

LIBRARIES OPERATE PURSUANT to a wide variety of federal and state laws, but arguably the most legally regulated aspect of library operations is its human resources activities. Administrators must comply with federal and state labor relations statutes, court cases interpreting those statutes, collective agreements in unionized institutions, and human resources policies and procedures which implement the laws. Like most administrators, my managerial experience began with overseeing a small library department and then moving to progressively larger units before administering an entire library. In this chapter, I will discuss three situations in which I developed an understanding of applicable laws and how they impacted me and my staff members.

ACCOMMODATIONS UNDER THE ADA

My first managerial experience was as the head of the acquisitions department of a special library at an Association of Research Libraries institution in the Midwest. I had a small staff of four employees, one of whom I will call Sarah,[1] the library's bindery clerk. As a new manager I was fortunate to have the opportunity to attend training sessions offered by the Human Resources Department to gain knowledge about, and confidence in dealing with, personnel matters. Some sessions focused on legal issues we might face, including sexual harassment, illegal interview questions, and accommodating a disability. Due to these sessions I understood what the law required of the employer, and this knowledge hopefully would help me identify the steps I should take if any of these legal issues arose.

I had worked as a reference librarian in the library for eighteen months before being promoted to the head of acquisitions, so I knew the staff members I was now supervising. I was aware that Sarah often acted in an immature manner notwithstanding the fact that she was in her forties. When I became the head of acquisitions, I reviewed the file that my predecessors had created on each of my staff members, which contained copies of all the annual evaluations and handwritten notes the former heads had made or had received from or about this employee.

About a year after I started as head of acquisitions, Sarah began exhibiting inappropriate behavior. She wandered around the library making a gun shape with her thumb and forefinger, pointing it at students and staff members and saying "bang bang." She thought this was funny and would often laugh after doing it. This behavior was made worse by its timing—just months after the Columbine school shooting. Actions that might have been previously laughed at now could have the appearance of being a threat.

I reported the behavior to my immediate supervisor, the library's assistant director, who suggested we seek guidance from our Human Resources advisor ("HR advisor") because she was not sure how seriously this should be treated. It was during the meeting with the HR advisor and assistant director that I learned for the first time that Sarah had a known neurological condition, with a letter from her neurologist in her official personnel file. I had not realized that my predecessors' file did not contain copies of all relevant personnel documents.

Given Sarah's known neurological impairment, the HR advisor summarized the key provisions of the Americans with Disabilities Act (ADA) for me: employers must make reasonable accommodations for employees with an impairment that limits one of the major life activities unless it would cause an undue hardship for the employer. The act did not require us to allow inappropriate and potentially threatening behavior to continue, however.

We considered the seriousness of Sarah's behavior to determine what action was warranted; some threatening behaviors could lead to dismissal. Looking at the picture as a whole, it was decided to initially take basic corrective action that involved me discussing the behavior with Sarah and providing her with an opportunity to cease the behavior. Sarah was initially very dismissive of the concerns I raised, saying no one could feel threatened by a hand shaped into a gun. To help her understand our new reality, I referenced the heightened tension at schools and universities since the Columbine shootings. I also showed her a newspaper article about a five-year-old boy being suspended for taking a toy gun to school to demonstrate the level of concern at all educational institutions. While she still argued with me, she agreed to and did cease the behavior.

What did I learn from this experience?

> Your predecessor's personnel files may not contain copies of all critical documents. Ask to see the official file to ensure you have a complete picture of personnel issues you have inherited.

> Determine whether any of your staff members have informed the library administration or Human Resources Department about a physical or mental impairment. This is especially important if there are no accommodations in place because, obviously, people are aware of impairments if someone has an accommodation. I followed my own advice in a subsequent position because one of my staff members' mannerisms led me to wonder if he had an impairment. After checking his official file, I saw that my predecessors had also wondered about the staff member and had even asked the Human Resources Department to verify if there was any documentation on his file that substantiated an actual impairment, which there wasn't.

AT-WILL EMPLOYEES, MEDICAL LEAVES, AND LAWSUITS

I had been a librarian for five years, with more than three years of managerial experience, when I became the head of public services for a stand-alone special library at a private university in a western state. The position of head of public services had been vacant for over a year when I arrived in early 2002 and my predecessor, who had been in the position for two decades, had allowed the librarians to independently determine the tasks they would perform and how to do them. Upon arriving, I met with each public services librarian and paraprofessional to understand their duties, how they performed them, and why. From these meetings, it became clear to me how inconsistently our services were being offered.

After gathering and analyzing the information on the services my librarians were offering and their capabilities for growth, I devised a strategy for increasing our services, identifying programs we could begin offering, and the potential roles each librarian could play. The library's director and I met with our HR advisor to discuss whether we could make the planned changes to the librarians' job responsibilities and the process we should undertake in this endeavor. The HR advisor confirmed that our librarians were at-will employees and we could change their duties as long as we were not taking these actions in a retaliatory manner.

One of the changes we made to my part-time reference librarian—I'll call her Elaine—was to eliminate her weekly two hours of telecommuting. My reasons for this were twofold: the project for which the telecommuting had been granted had concluded, and we needed her to increase her hours on the reference desk. Human Resources confirmed that we were within our rights to stop her telecommuting hours due to these operational needs. Elaine was extremely upset about the elimination of her telecommunication time, but she verbally agreed to her change of hours by the end of our meeting with her.

Notwithstanding her verbal agreement, Elaine demonstrated her unhappiness the next week by informing me via an e-mail that she would not be in at all that week due to medical appointments for doctors located two hours' away in Elaine's hometown, when she knew we were short-handed due to summer vacations. An important missing piece of the puzzle is that Elaine had been diagnosed with a potentially debilitating disease a couple of years before my arrival. She had verbally told the director and then me about the disease but had asked both of us to not inform anyone else; she had not informed Human Resources nor was she exhibiting any symptoms relating to the disease. She did not request any time off due to the disease (except for the occasional medical appointment) either before or after my arrival—until we changed her hours of work.

My director and I met with our HR advisor for guidance on how to respond to Elaine's e-mail. She suggested that we send Elaine a letter outlining the procedures she was to use when requesting time off for medical appointments, confirming the elimination of her telecommuting hours, and summarizing her new duties. The HR advisor provided the wording for the letter and we used it though we were both concerned that it was impersonal, quite firm, and perhaps even harsh. Elaine's response to the letter was to seek legal advice and sue the institution. Elaine's lawsuit claimed that my director and I had improperly removed a previously approved accommodation (her telecommuting) and failed to provide her with a requested medical leave under both the Family Medical Leave Act and a state statute. The Family Medical Leave Act is designed to protect individuals with serious medical conditions by requiring employers to provide employees with time off for personal illness. The act also protects employees from employers taking actions against them in retaliation or discriminating against them for exercising their statutory rights. Elaine alleged that the letter we sent was retaliation to her request for time off to attend her medical appointments.

The first step after the institution was served with Elaine's suit was for my director and I to meet with the university's lawyer and explain what had transpired from our perspective. Both the director and I were then served with a request for interrogatories (which are questions we had to answer in writing) and were required to provide copies of e-mails and other documents related to this matter. It is critical to review any notes and documentation you have when answering the interrogatories and to admit when you are unsure of something because you may later be questioned on these matters under oath during depositions or at trial, and your interrogatories' answers could be used against you. Indeed, the next step in the lawsuit was a request for each of us to be deposed. Depositions involve answering a series of oral questions asked by the lawyer representing the other party while under oath. Our lawyer met with us before the depositions and provided us with guidance on how to respond to the questions—he instructed us in the tone of voice we should use and the manner in which we were to respond to the questions but not the information we were to provide for each answer. He advised us to (1) think about each question prior to answering it, (2) tell the truth, (3) answer just the question asked but not provide additional information, and (4) to not answer in a defensive or argumentative tone.

While the library director and I were the only individuals from the institution specifically named in Elaine's court documents, we were not "our" lawyer's clients—the university was. This was brought home a few months after the completion of depositions when I learned that my employer had settled the lawsuit—not because our lawyer felt we would lose at trial but because Elaine had agreed to a sum that was significantly less than the estimated cost of going to trial. I found it emotionally difficult to accept the settlement because it felt like an admission that I had done something wrong, even though I understood the cost savings argument.

What did I learn from this experience?

> Keep records! I was very fortunate that Elaine's lawsuit was filed so quickly that the events were still fresh in my mind. Lawsuits can be filed years after the cause of action arises, however, which could make relying on your memory very difficult. Having notes written during or immediately after a meeting can help you remember dates and the order of important events. "Contemporaneous records," as these notes are called, make it difficult for the other party to contend that something else was said or done.

> Do not take legal claims or lawsuits personally. Lawyers are hired to represent their client's best interests and make claims necessary to achieve their purpose. This may also mean that your lawyer

may recommend actions that you do not agree with although they are best for the university.

Rely on your lawyer for advice on how to act if a lawsuit if filed. He is hired to represent what is best for the institution in these circumstances and this aligns with what is best for you professionally, although it sometimes might not feel best for you personally from an emotional perspective.

UNIONS AND COLLECTIVE AGREEMENTS

My third position was director of a special library at a Canadian Association of Research Libraries institution. The university's nonacademic staff members belong to a provincewide union and its academic staff, including the librarians, are members of the faculty association, which also has a collective agreement with the university. Collective agreements are negotiated, binding legal documents which govern the relationship between the employer (the university) and the employee, and any staffing changes must be made in accordance with the agreements. I read the collective agreements when I started at the university to make sure I understood what I was able or required to do as a manager. I subsequently learned, however, that politics can limit the actions managers would be allowed to take under these agreements.

Less than a year after my arrival, all administrators were asked to consider workforce reductions. I identified two positions whose duties could be absorbed by the remaining staff members so their abolishment would not significantly impact our operation. One of the positions was that of the library's assistant director, a librarian position, and the other position was a library assistant position. I soon realized there would be no financial savings from eliminating the assistant director position because the librarian had tenure and so I abandoned that idea.

We did, however, begin the process of abolishing the library assistant position, but ultimately this process was also halted—but for political, not legal, reasons. I met with our HR advisor and one of the university's labor relations specialists—an individual in the Human Resources Department who specializes in the application of the collective agreements, and who interacts with the union and faculty association on behalf of the university—to discuss the position's abolishment. While in theory I knew the process involved in the position's abolishment, they were able to explain how it would actually be carried out and how "bumping" worked under the collective agreement. Essentially, bumping allows the individual whose position is being abolished to take the position of any more junior individual in a similar position of equal or lower classification within the same bargaining unit. While my library assistant could not bump any staff members in my library, there were several people in other units in the library system (which is counted as one bargaining unit) that he could have bumped. Tensions developed when the directors of other library units realized which staff members they might lose through my position abolishment. Due to the ripple effect on other units in the library system, it was ultimately decided not to abolish the library assistant position; instead, library student assistant hours were cut in another unit and the library assistant began performing those tasks, which resulted in a small financial savings.

Eighteen months after my arrival, I was promoted to the equivalent of an associate university librarian position. As with my other positions, I was given the mandate of implementing change, including updating the liaison assignments of our academic staff. The collective agreement between the faculty association and the university allowed for changes to be made to a librarian's position as long as the individual had been consulted. After determining the changes needed, we met with the impacted librarians several times and discussed the changes. After we announced the changes, the librarians expressed their dissatisfaction with their new responsibilities to the faculty association. When informed by the faculty association that the librarians might file an official grievance over this, senior administration would not stand firm on the decision, even though my actions complied with the mandate I had been given and every step I took had been preapproved by the administration. We were informed that, notwithstanding the lack of a requirement that the librarian consent to the change of responsibilities, human resources insisted on their agreement and was not willing to fight with the faculty association over this matter.

What did I learn from this experience?

> You cannot assume that collective agreements will be strictly interpreted and enforced. You should determine from human resources in advance how they apply relevant provisions and how you should proceed.
>
> Internal politics may also impact legal personnel actions you want to take. You need to consider whether your plans may impact other units in the library system and consult affected managers.

Managers must be familiar with labor relations laws because they govern the relationship between the administration and the employees. Human resources departments are excellent sources of information—either through courses or by providing advice when a situation arises. There are also several books that discuss how personnel laws apply to academic libraries that could be consulted.[2] However, as with most skills, you learn how to act pursuant to these laws when faced with a situation that forces you to do so. Experience truly is the best teacher.

NOTES

1. The names of all individuals have been changed to protect their privacy.
2. See, for example, David A. Baldwin, *The Academic Librarian's Human Resources Handbook: Employer Rights and Responsibilities* (Englewood, CO: Libraries Unlimited, 1996); Janice Simmons-Welburn and Beth McNeil, eds., *Human Resource Management in Today's Academic Library: Meeting Challenges and Creating Opportunities* (Westport, CT: Libraries Unlimited, 2004); and Ronald R. Sims, *Legal and Regulatory Issues in Human Resources Management* (Charlotte, NC: Information Age Publishing, 2014).

THERESA LIEDTKA and
VIRGINIA CAIRNS

8

Facilities for the Director

Communication and Process

LIBRARIANS, LEADERSHIP, AND FACILITIES are not words that you frequently find together. Yet a quick scan of journals and discussion lists demonstrates that library facilities are now receiving the attention that library collections have received for decades. As the concept of library as place has grown in popularity, new threads in the conversation include shrinking print collections, the adoption of user-centered design principles, the development of new services such as maker spaces, and organizational mergers with related student support services such as writing and communication centers, tutoring, and supplemental instruction. As buildings have become more multifaceted and technology-rich, facilities management skills have become a critical aspect of library leadership. These skills are rarely even mentioned in library school, so many managers have had little or no exposure to knowledge or experience in this area. With that understanding in mind, this chapter seeks to outline practical approaches to successful library facilities management that can be applied to daily operations as well as more substantive changes such as space renovations or new construction.

THE INNER CIRCLE: ROUTINE BUILDING OPERATIONS

Managing Daily Access, Maintenance, and Operational Issues

It takes people to bring a facility to life, to tend and manage it much like a garden. On a day-to-day basis, the smooth and efficient operation of your building is going to fall on the shoulders of a few key staff members who deal directly with the facility and its operations. This inner circle of library staff members is the first line of problem reporting, problem tracking, and problem solving. The size of your building and its operation will impact the number of individuals involved. Library administration is always a member of the inner circle, as are information technology staff and assorted key public services positions, such as building openers and closers. While there is an inner circle of library staff members who are directly responsible for the building, ulti- mately all library staff must take responsibility for reporting building prob- lems when they observe or experience them. With this expectation clearly established, it is the library administration's responsibility to create a simple and efficient mechanism for staff to report on and track problems in place.

> **TIP**
> Set up a number of e-mail distribution lists that copy various groups of key employees who can evaluate and respond promptly to building issues of various types. This will greatly improve awareness and response time because multiple people are made aware of an issue in a timely manner.

In addition to routine problem reporting, effective building maintenance involves constant vigilance for developing issues. At least one daily walk- through is important to make sure that doors, restrooms, lighting, HVAC (heating, ventilating, and air conditioning), furnishings, and other physical aspects of the building are all in good working order. In some libraries, the morning opener walks the building and will note any wear and tear that needs to be addressed. In larger buildings, a library facility staff member will devote time each day to a thorough building inspection because the library's square footage is significantly larger and opening staff may not have time to visit all areas or notice minor issues.

> **TIP**
> Develop a short web form that allows the openers, closers, and facility specialists to report issues discovered on walk-throughs. Multiple forms may be useful, or one form can combine reporting for maintenance, cleaning, security, information technology, and other building issues.

Communication and record keeping are two critical areas of focus. It is one thing to report a problem and make others aware of it; it is another to put processes in place that allow for easy record keeping and follow-up. An internal library blog is a good way to inform all building staff members that a problem has been reported. For example, if an elevator is out of order, multiple staff members are likely to report it. A library-wide blog post is one way to inform all staff that a problem has been reported, as well as to date stamp the reporting of the problem. Such a blog is also useful for noting unexpected absences and other key library-wide events. It is further recommended that a simple database or spreadsheet be developed to record reported problems and keep track of repair issues and frequency. Such a spreadsheet would allow for a detailed analysis of problems and their associated costs.

> **TIP**
>
> Develop an internal library-wide or building blog and post all known building problems to it. Implement a problem-tracking mechanism to allow for easy follow-up as well as detailed analysis of building problems and issues.

In facility management there are multiple opportunities to make use of formal groups (committees and task forces) to improve processes, clarify and affirm policy, and respond to concerns. In this arena, the use of a standing committee devoted to building use is common. For example, this group of staff members can codify facility use policies pertaining to building access and building conduct, and can affirm that policies are posted publicly for patrons and for staff to refer to. Safety and emergency preparedness are sometimes under the purview of a facilities committee, or such preparedness may involve a separate task force. Many of the other decision-making areas referred to in this chapter can be handled via such a group—cleaning contracts, security in a 24-hour space, rules and boundaries for room usage by groups, and so on.

> **TIP**
>
> Establish a library-wide building use or facility committee that is charged with managing daily policy and process matters. Tasks such as emergency preparedness or development of a memorandum of understanding or cleaning contract can fall to special task forces or this group.

THE SECOND CIRCLE: BUILDING TENANTS

Managing Relationships with Internal Partners

Most university libraries are not islands because they live and work closely with building partners; for example, campus writing centers are now more commonly found in libraries, as are information technology-related help desks. In some cases the partnership is a result of nothing more than location proximity, while in other cases the partnership is mission driven.

The co-location of student support services in library buildings has become a trend in recent years. Many libraries have moved closer to a model of the "one stop shop" for needs such as tutoring, advising, writing, faculty development, and even IT support. Sharing a physical space with many different groups that do not report to the library administration can present a unique set of challenges for library leaders. This is an instance where shared expectations need to be established and open lines of communication are essential. A process that is commonly used to delineate the boundaries of a co-location arrangement is a memorandum of understanding (MOU). Decisions need to be made about a wide range of concerns ranging from building access to participation in emergency response plans. The preparation and implementation of an MOU is the most efficient means of providing answers to these sorts of building-related questions. It is possible to locate sample MOUs on the Web and library discussion lists, so do not reinvent the wheel in crafting your own. Local details will need to be tweaked, particularly with respect to things like responding to emergencies or on-boarding a new staff member, but the overarching areas that need to be addressed are usually outlined in sample documents. Once an MOU is signed and adopted, it should be revisited occasionally to ensure that it remains current and any new concerns that arise are addressed.

TIP

Develop a memorandum of understanding or MOU with building partners to ensure the clarity of building processes and procedures.

Success in managing a building also requires good communication between the library administration and the managers of the various building tenants. A mission-driven building partnership can serve to benefit students through shared learning and increased understanding of partner operations. Relationships start in the on-boarding phase, continue through routine daily life, and end with off-boarding. The library administration should work with internal building managers on managing these life cycles and relationships. Techniques that work to create positive building partnerships can include central problem reporting, clear building access procedures, and building-wide meetings or

TIP

Develop an on-boarding process and communication plan for building tenant staff to ensure that they have a clear understanding of building access and operational issues. Provide ongoing building-wide learning and sharing opportunities such as orientations, monthly meetings and presentations, emergency response trainings, and more.

training sessions as a means of ensuring building awareness and the promotion of productive partner conversations.

THE THIRD CIRCLE: BUILDING PARTNERS

Managing Relationships with Cleaning and Maintenance, Information Technology, Risk Management, and Security

As we move beyond library staff members and building residents, partnerships become more operational in nature; for example, working with campus security to close the library building each night. These partners represent the third circle of building management and are absolutely essential to the success of library operations. Third-circle partners are those that handle ongoing building demands and include facility cleaning and maintenance, information technology, and risk management and security.

Facility Cleaning and Maintenance

Cleanliness is perhaps the most relentless aspect of library building management, depending on your building policies. A library that does not allow food or drink in the building will have a different experience from a library that does. In general, though, libraries are high-traffic, people-dense buildings that are open very long hours for most of the year. As a result, they need constant attention: restrooms, floors, trash, recycling, tabletops, seating, and windows, just to name a few. The parent institution sometimes provides custodial services or they may be provided by an outside company, but either way they are an essential part of facilities management. Regardless of the custodial model employed, it is absolutely essential to develop strong and positive relationships with the cleaning crew and to have the cleaning specifications for your building spelled out in great detail. It can be helpful to walk the entire building room by room and note every single surface and zone to be cleaned and to indicate the frequency and products to be used, if possible. If an external company is handling your cleaning, then the request for proposal should be detailed to the nth degree, itemizing tasks and levels of cleanliness at the outset. Time frames for cleaning are also crucial to establish up front, since most cleaning in the library will have to take place after hours when the building is empty of patrons.

TIP

Prepare a building cleaning and maintenance checklist to create a shared understanding of cleaning routines, communication expectations, and expected outcomes.

Establishing custodial standards and expectations up front makes for a clear understanding and gives library managers something to point to if service is substandard. It is often a wise practice to have one person (usually in the administration or in access services) serve as the point of contact between the library and the cleaning crew or their supervisor. This is another instance where an e-mail distribution list is useful. This gives everyone in the building an easy means of reporting cleaning issues and the point person (and his backup) can direct requests appropriately and keep track of follow-through. Obviously, for minor emergencies like spills or clogged toilets, short-term plans should be made to triage the situation until cleaners can get to the scene (and their response time will vary depending on the time of day).

> **TIP**
>
> Use a distribution list for reporting cleaning problems and appoint a point person to routinely communicate on building cleanliness issues.

Along the same lines as custodial services, library managers need to establish strong working relationships with other campus departments that provide support for building operations. The campus facilities department is such a department. Between the usual maintenance needs that all buildings require such as plumbing, wiring, and HVAC up to and including other high-tech systems such as programmable lighting, card swipes, and patrons' counters, there is a very long list of potential problems that will need to be reported accurately and tracked closely. Given the complexities of many of these newer building systems, issues may arise that are difficult to describe, replicate, or diagnose. This aspect of facilities management calls for thorough and careful documentation, open communication, and persistence. With regard to communication, it is essential that library managers speak up and ask for information and a voice in the process of diagnosing and resolving maintenance problems. After all, library staff live in the building and are the ones most familiar with its operations. It is also important to ask for specific training to facilitate the library's role in managing and maintaining various systems. Solid plans should also be made for contacting facilities help after hours and on weekends.

> **TIP**
>
> Request training and documentation on all building facilities and develop routine and after-hour reporting procedures.

Information Technology

The maintenance of networking and IT infrastructure is every bit as important as the maintenance of the electrical or HVAC systems. Libraries have become almost completely technology-dependent organizations, and it is crucial that connectivity and networking remain stable and seamless. Libraries are usually dependent on campus IT for networking, server, storage, identity management issues, and enterprise systems. Even in libraries that have their own independent IT departments, a close working relationship with campus IT will be essential in order to ensure that larger problems involving the campus network or connectivity to the local Internet backbone will be resolved quickly. Developing triage plans and emergency contact lists are an important step that will allow front-line personnel to reach the appropriate person when assistance is needed for reporting an outage or resolving a problem. Libraries can be important partners for campus IT as well. Library IT can participate in configuring and testing new services and software, working out the kinks encountered in going live. Library IT staff can also be valuable advocates when serving on campus work groups or committees, articulating the technology needs of students and faculty based on their experience on the front lines. As with any collaborative arrangement, an equal partnership that works both ways is advantageous to both parties.

> **TIP**
>
> Request training and documentation on all information technology systems, and develop routine and after-hours reporting procedures.

Risk Management and Security

Perhaps the most high-profile concern within this third circle of campus partners would be the relationship with campus security and risk management. In most cases, the point people in your library for handling contact with security personnel will be the staff members who work in circulation or administration. Circulation staff members, or staff members at a like-desk, report after-hour problems as they open or close the building and provide coverage at the service point that is open the longest hours into the evenings and on weekends. The library administration may report issues during business hours. Regular conversation with law enforcement officers conducting daily patrols through buildings provides the basis for a strong collaborative relationship. Frequent communication will help promote a quick response and smooth coordination between the library and security when an unexpected disruptive event occurs.

> **TIP**
>
> Develop clear communication protocols and processes for reporting both routine and unusual security concerns.

Strong emergency planning and disaster response training go hand in hand with a good security presence to affirm a high level of building safety. A sound emergency plan should be implemented with thorough staff training, and reviewed annually. Training should include actual participation in drills on the proper responses to various types of unforeseen events. Templates for such plans can easily be found on the Web and can be adapted to match the circumstances at any given institution. Training is often offered on campus or through local emergency preparedness agencies. Finally, locating brief one-page "emergency response reminders" at each service desk will make the appropriate response easier to carry out in the event that staff feel uncertain how to proceed. Risk management personnel will also be familiar with your local fire suppression systems and should pass along relevant information to front-line library personnel to be used in the event of an emergency.

> **TIP**
>
> Develop a building emergency response plan, as well as a one-page summary posted in local departments and at service desks.

THE FOURTH CIRCLE: MANAGING BUILDING AND RENOVATION PROJECTS

Working with Architects, Design Teams, and Planning Committees

The fourth or outer circle is the final circle and involves substantial renovations or building projects. The cast of characters can include internal players as well as specific professionals brought in to work on the project, including architects, interior designers, and construction firms and subcontractors. The complexities of managing a renovation or construction project can be very daunting, but there are a few strategies that can be used to keep the process moving forward and focused on the best possible outcome.

The individuals and groups you will be called on to work with during renovation or construction projects include architects, interior designers, construction firms, subcontractors for areas such as signage, acoustics, green practices, and site engineering, campus officials and executives, and in most cases some form of advisory committee of campus stakeholders. Working with architects and engineers comes with a certain learning curve. They often seem to speak a different language, and the questions and concerns they bring to the table are often things librarians have not considered. This educational process must also be two-way. Few architects are familiar with libraries and their practices. It is crucial that librarians explain patron needs and core services and advocate strongly for designs and spaces that serve those needs. Gorgeous, soaring atriums may be appealing from an architectural perspective, but they are often not what works best for a library. Traffic patterns and library security require all patrons to enter and exit through a small number of choke points, which may be a foreign concept to an architect accustomed to designing other types of public buildings. Lots of conversation and discussion between library staff and designers must take place in order for a shared understanding to be reached and a patron-friendly library to be constructed. Develop realistic time lines and communicate them to everyone repeatedly. Leading a building project requires a certain amount of the taskmaster approach. Communicate deadlines and then also follow up and insist that group members stick to them.

> **TIP**
>
> A shared understanding of needs and expectations between librarians and architects is essential for a successful building or renovation project.

When beginning a renovation or new building, the best first step is to collect input. Survey your patrons, hold focus groups, invite stakeholders to visioning sessions, read the professional literature, search the Web for designs and images, and conduct site visits at a variety of libraries within driving distance of your location. The more information you collect, the stronger your design decisions will be. As you begin to lay out the spaces in your building, learn to consider adjacencies. Where should the media studio be located? Where do you want your staff offices located? How many service desks do you need? Where are the best locations for those desks? Workflows often drive design decisions about staff work spaces, so be certain you are thinking ahead to the future and not basing decisions on the way things were done twenty years ago when your current office space was designed. When searching for furnishings, get samples of many different pieces and have users actually test them for comfort and ease of use. Do whatever you can to ensure that your design process is hands-on and user-focused. When making site visits, photograph everything extensively and select the details and configurations that you believe would work best for your patrons.

> **TIP**
>
> Gather as much input as possible for your building or renovation project.

As you collect this wealth of data, be sure to develop an online home base to store it all for documentation and sharing. Build a wiki or a shared space (Google Drive or Dropbox) to house all your information and ensure that it is easily accessible to everyone involved in the project. Wikis allow for organizational hierarchies and easily searchable text files as well as storage locations for photos, design plans, slide shows, or videos. Shared drives allow for sharing and simultaneous editing. Down the road when you need to track down the most recent furniture layout diagram, it will be far easier if you have done the legwork at the outset to create a structured repository for all of your documentation.

> **TIP**
>
> Develop and implement an accessible and reliable document storage system.

When planning a large-scale project like a renovation or building program, multiple groups may be needed to divide and conquer the many pieces and parts of the overall process. Both internal and external building committees are often needed. They can serve as planning committees, policy committees, or both. Carefully selecting group members who can represent a wide variety of perspectives from alumni to faculty to members of the local community can do much to ensure widespread support and forward progress. Some possible committees encountered during a building or renovation project might include

> **Internal Building or Renovation Project Committee:** The core group that will accomplish most of the detailed planning. If a new dedicated committee is not formed, an existing library management committee can serve in this role.

> **External Building or Renovation Project Committee:** Offering an outside perspective and serving primarily in an advisory role, this group can include a wider variety of players. If a new dedicated committee is not formed, an existing campus facilities group may be able to serve in this role.

> **TIP**
>
> Use committees judiciously to successfully manage renovation and building projects. Don't be afraid to appoint small subcommittees to complete focused tasks like the development of a service model.

CONCLUSION

Running a successful library facility is a hard but not insurmountable task. From a leadership perspective, it comes down to focusing on people, practicing open communication, and developing solid processes. First and foremost, library staff members are at the center of the building process. Secondary to the people come the carefully crafted internal policies and processes that function collectively as the support framework for successful facility management. The third aspect is open and proactive communication among all parties to ensure a clear, shared understanding of procedures and expectations. With these three facets working together, managing a library building becomes a much more efficient process.

LISA BEINHOFF

9
Library Safety and Security

AS I WRITE THIS, I can hear the echoes of the blast waves from major bomb and ordnance detonations that are currently taking place miles away on campus at the Energetic Materials Research and Testing Center (EMRTC), the bomb range and missile detonation site which is affiliated with my university. Since the New Mexico Institute of Mining and Technology is one of the few universities that offers degrees with a specialization in explosives engineering, offers an explosives summer camp for high school students, and gives students the opportunity to blow up their textbooks at the end of the semester, not too surprisingly it is also the only campus I have been on that receives a credible bomb threat every few years.

What this illustrates is that every campus is different and has a unique set of pertinent safety issues. One of the first tasks set before any new library director is to identify, prioritize, assess, plan, and respond to the most pressing safety challenges presented by his or her specific campus. Whether your campus is in an urban or rural area, what the crime rate in the neighborhood around the campus is, and whether the campus is located in an area susceptible to natural disasters are all factors to consider when prioritizing which safety issues need to be dealt with first. Perhaps the most irksome part of dealing with safety issues is the fact that dealing with these issues is a constant and ongoing process, which should never end. Forming a committee to prepare and plan for a specific issue; documenting the library's policies and procedures for dealing with the safety issue in question; going through the process of training and preparing library staff to execute the library's plan; responding to the safety issue and mitigating the damage caused by a safety incident; debriefing and recovering from the safety challenge; and starting the entire process over from the beginning when the nature of the safety issue changes are daunting processes at best.

In general, the safety issues that a library director needs to prepare for, plan for, respond to, and protect the library from fall into three categories: problem patrons, illegal/criminal acts, and emergencies/disasters. In all three cases, the library director is always trying to protect people, tangible property, buildings, and virtual property,[1] or some combination thereof.[2] For many authors on academic library safety, library safety issues are far more multi-dimensional than is expressed by these three categories. Shuman[3] breaks down library safety into building security, equipment security, materials security, personal safety, personal comfort, financial liability, legal issues, problem patrons, ethical issues, and electronic security. Kahn[4] focuses on what is being protected: the building, the collections, the materials, and the people, short-shifting those issues that lap into multiple areas. Still others[5] only address specific security issues without putting them into any context.

However, as a library director, I have found it best to employ a simple three-pronged schema to categorize library safety issues and assess what will be involved in addressing each type of issue. In general, problem patron issues are any safety issue that involves the people who use the library (and sometimes the library's staff members), and which does not involve the direct violation of a campus, federal, or state law. Examples of issues that fall into this category include rules about patron access to library "staff only" areas, key control practices, patron privacy issues, proxy server security issues, actions to be taken to curtail mildly disruptive behaviors, restrictions that aim to limit the abuse of library equipment, DVD security practices, rules about loitering, and policies about soliciting. Though troublesome, problem patron issues are relatively minor and are easy for the library to recover from.

Unfortunately, it is not uncommon for a patron problem to escalate into an illegal/criminal act, thus blurring the line between how to deal with a specific safety issue. For instance, the library staff members may apply a lenient problem patron policy to deal with patrons having a heated verbal argument. However, if the patrons in the heated argument start punching each other, the incident quickly escalates into a criminal act and the library staff members can no longer apply the library's lenient policy because the incident is now a matter for the campus police force.

PATRON PROBLEMS

Because patron problems are the most common safety issues, dealing with them will also draw the lion's share of a new library director's effort. As a rule, patron problems should be dealt with well in advance of the safety issue actually occurring. This means that the library's policy creation, planning, and preventive measures all need to happen before the problem occurs; and the coordinated mitigation and response of the library's staff members to an incident should happen after the problem occurs. In reality, it is far more common to have a problem or incident with a patron occur, and then to have the library director scramble around retroactively creating a policy to deal with the patron problem. Though reactive policy creation may seem to be as effective as preemptive policy creation, the library director needs to understand that reversing the order in which a policy is created is inherently risky.

By having the library's staff acting without policies, there is a chance that a library staff member dealing with a problem patron may act incorrectly and cause collateral damage. There is also a chance that the patron problem will go uncorrected, setting a precedent for the problem to occur again or to escalate in the future. Lastly, there is a chance that the patron causing the problem will interpret the creation and enforcement of the library's new policy as a personal attack. It should be noted that having a library patron interpret a library policy change as a personal attack can be particularly destructive to both the reputation of the library director and the reputation of the institution, especially if that patron who feels attacked happens to be a member of a minority group.

There are many issues that need to be considered when creating a fair and equitable problem patron policy which protects the library, prevents the problem from happening, deals with ethical issues, deals with legal issues, and mitigates the damage to all parties involved if and when the patron problem actually occurs. For instance, the last two campuses that I worked at both had safety issues involving the combination of having a registered sexual offender using the library and having unattended children in the library. As a result, each campus was in immediate need of an enforceable "children in the library" policy.

Unlike some public libraries, which can legally limit a registered sexual offender's library access,[6] academic libraries do not have the right to restrict registered sex offenders from using the library facility unless they are actively violating a university policy. In addition, because of his or her status as a registered sexual offender, the person can often have trouble becoming employed and commonly will become a student seeking an academic degree in order to improve his or her employability.[7] At both campuses the library staff members had identified multiple known registered sex offenders who had previously been convicted of offenses against minors, and who spent a good portion of their week in the library.

As with all safety issues, the rights of all parties needed to be balanced while protecting the library. Registered sexual offenders (even when their offenses involved children) have the legal right to use an academic library. They have the right not to be harassed, followed, constantly watched, or questioned, despite the wishes of some library staff members. And just because they have had previous convictions, this does not mean that they are likely to immediately perpetrate the same crime again in the library.

On the other hand, people have the right to bring their children with them to the library. Unfortunately, many people with children are blissfully unaware that academic libraries are not "safe zones" like public libraries. Public libraries are designed to serve children. They have designated "children" and "teen" areas, have staff trained to deal with children, and have collections designed for children. But even though public libraries purposefully cater to children, people often treat them as day-care facilities, leaving their children in the library unattended for hours.[8] In the case of the academic library, many students and faculty members alike often wrongly view the academic library as a "safe zone" and will park their children in an empty carrel or study room while they go to class. The question of providing unmediated Internet access to minors also needed to be considered when crafting this policy. Many college campuses do not filter or otherwise curtail Internet use in any way. Since many a child has his or her own Wi-Fi-enabled device, a child in an academic library can easily connect to the Internet, and may access inappropriate material.

Because entire floors of academic libraries are often unstaffed and study rooms are often soundproof, more lenient public library policies, which allow children to remain unattended for an hour or two,[9] are unacceptable for an academic library. The failure to have an adequate and enforced policy can often result in the library functioning as an impromptu child-care service, which puts both the library and the library's director in a legally indefensible position. Conversely, notifying the library's users that the library is an unsafe place is also unacceptable. If one advertises that a known registered sex offender hangs out in your library, one hurts the library's public relations with the community, and violates the rights of the library's patrons to privacy. Because of all these considerations, the final policies set at both libraries were similar.

The base components of both policies included

1. Definition of who is a child.[10]

2. Unequivocal statement that anyone with child status must be under the direct supervision of an adult at all times.

3. A disclosure about the library's lack of filtering software on its Internet connections, and the adult's responsibility for monitoring a child's Internet activity.[11]

4. A statement that unacceptable behavior will result in the child's expulsion from the library.

By creating these policies cooperatively with library staff members and having all library employees uniformly enforce these policies, libraries protect the children visiting the library, respect the rights of people without children to use the library, and avoid having any major incidents involving children in the library. Surprisingly enough, the first "children in the library policy" that I had to create did not start out as a policy about children, but instead started out as a "registered sex offenders in the library policy," which was initiated at the request of the library's circulation staff. However, after careful consideration about who the library's primary clientele were, the topic of the policy was changed. Since college students and faculty members are the primary patrons served by academic libraries, the rights of anyone who is a student or faculty member take precedence over the rights of anyone who is not, such as a child.

This illustrates a common trap that the new library director can fall into, which is being brought one safety issue in the guise of another safety issue. In this case, what at first appeared to be an illegal/criminal act issue for one user group was actually a patron safety issue for a totally different user group. Determining what kind of safety issue one is dealing with is important, because each specific type of safety issue requires input from a different set of people in order to be properly addressed. Depending on the type of safety problem being dealt with and what is being protected, the committee that the library director needs to assemble to create and implement a policy may include staff members from different departments in the library, institutional employees from different campus divisions outside of the library, and even officials from agencies outside of the campus community.

For instance, problem patron issues which only involve people, physical property, or the library building itself usually only require input from the library's staff. In the case of problem patron issues, which involve virtual property (e.g., electronic database journal subscriptions, e-books, computer servers, etc.), it will be necessary for the campus's information technology department or computing services department to become involved in the policy's creation along with the library's staff.

ILLEGAL CRIMINAL ACTS

Preparing the library to deal with illegal/criminal acts can require either a little or a lot of input from campus police, depending on whether the library chooses to follow standard campus procedures. If the library director chooses to fully adopt campus policies, or only adds a few steps to noncritical portions of the policy, the process of policy creation can be relatively simple. However, if the library director chooses to create policies that diverge from campuswide policies and procedures (possibly to protect patron privacy), the process of creating these policies becomes far more complex and will have to include both campus police and the library staff.

Though safety issues that constitute illegal/criminal acts may require very little new policy creation, they do require far more investment by the library staff in the process of preparing and recovering from these acts. Incidents like stalking, physical violence, sexual acts, drug use, alcohol consumption, and vandalism all fall into the category of illegal/criminal acts. Because the ramifications of illegal/criminal acts can be dire, it follows that poor preparation on the part of the library staff can have disastrous results. Staff meetings need to take place to review campuswide policies. An effort needs to be made to expeditiously notify campus police when criminal incidents take place. Simple hand motions and "code words" need to be established to covertly signal to other library staff members that there is trouble in a public area, so they can call the campus police when staff in the public areas are not able to do so. Preemptive safety measures like the installation of cameras, installation of panic buttons, and instituting required FERPA training[12] for all staff members may need to take place. And after an incident occurs, staff members will have to meet and debrief in order to evaluate the effectiveness of the library's preparedness plan.

The library director may also have to review and/or enhance existing campuswide safety policies in order to be prepared to deal with illegal/criminal acts. For instance, if one of the library building's windows gets broken, campus police would need to be called, a police report will need to be filed, and campus facilities would need to send someone to board up the window. The only additional steps that would be absolutely necessary at the time of the incident will be for the library director or the stack maintenance person to be notified, and for the books near the broken window to be shrouded in plastic to ensure that they will not get damaged if it rains.

EMERGENCIES/DISASTERS

Unlike patron safety issues and illegal/criminal acts, emergency/disaster safety issues are the most thankless ones to address, since the likelihood of their occurrence is the most remote. Conversely, failing to prepare for these safety incidents can be the most damaging to the library. It takes a lot of time to craft a usable policy, preemptively mitigate damage to the library's infrastructure, prepare staff to act quickly, have the staff practice responding to a simulated situation, use feedback from simulations to hone library procedures, respond to an actual situation, mitigate damage, and recover from the incident. Even detailed campuswide policies created by the institution's emergency preparedness committees will need far more than just minor customization in order to meet the needs of the library.

Just the act of creating policies and procedures that deal with disasters/emergencies is a highly collaborative activity which requires a larger number of constituents and extensive coordination between the library, facilities management, campus police, the local NIMS[13] personnel, and the administrators in charge of disaster response. Unlike the other two types of safety issues identified, emergencies/disasters are safety issues that may involve substantial damage to the library's materials and/or building. As a rule, all library materials and equipment are particularly susceptible to water damage, and any incident that involves water entering the library building can quickly become exponentially expensive. In order to minimize water damage, decisive actions are always necessary. Books that are waterlogged need immediate attention[14] and library servers and computers need to be saved.[15] Floods, hurricanes, tornados, earthquakes, fires, and bombings are all examples of possible disasters that can allow water into a library building. Other types of emergencies/disasters like epidemics, radiation leaks, and acts of terrorism are examples of disasters that may cause the library building to be left unattended for an extended period of time and susceptible to water infiltration.

Regardless of whether one is dealing with a patron problem, a criminal/illegal act, or preparing for a full-blown disaster/emergency, the process of dealing with safety issues is long and involved. The wise library director picks his or her battles and only deals with one or two safety issues at a time. The trick is to be able to prioritize the safety issues faced by the library, and to make sure to address first those safety issues that are the most likely to occur. By properly prioritizing, the library director should be able to plan for, prevent, and protect the library from those safety issues that are most likely to happen. And when an incident does occur, safety preparedness expedites the library preparing, mitigating, responding to, and recovering from these occurrences as quickly as possible.

NOTES

1. Virtual property includes computers, computer networks, servers, electronic subscriptions, patron information, library catalogs, discovery services, database subscriptions, and so on.
2. Bruce A. Shuman, *Library Security and Safety Handbook: Prevention, Policies, and Procedures* (Chicago: American Library Association, 1999), 14, http://search.ebscohost.com/login.aspx?direct=true&scope=site&db=nlebk&db=nlabk&AN=45110.
3. Ibid., 14.
4. Miriam Kahn, *Library Security and Safety Guide to Prevention, Planning, and Response* (Chicago: American Library Association, 2007); ProQuest ebrary, Web, iii.
5. *The Complete Library Safety and Security Manual: A Comprehensive Resource Manual for Academic and Public Library Professionals and Law Enforcement Officers* (Goshen, KY: Campus Crime Prevention Programs, 1998), i.
6. In Iowa, it is up to the public library administrator to determine whether a sexual offender is allowed to be in the library. Jacquelyn M. Meirick, "Through the Tiers:

Are Iowa's New Sex-Offender Laws Unconstitutional?" *Iowa Law Review* 96, no. 3 (2011): 1013–35; *OmniFile Full Text Select* (H.W. Wilson), Web, 1034.

7. Connor David and Richard Tewksbury, "Ex-Offenders and Educational Equal Access: Doctoral Programs in Criminology and Criminal Justice," *Critical Criminology* 20, no. 3 (September 2012): 327–40; ProQuest Theses and Dissertation Abstracts, Web, 328.

8. Claire B. Gunnels, Patricia M. Butler, and Susan E. Green, *Joint Libraries: Models That Work* (Chicago: American Library Association, 2012); *eBook Collection* (EBSCOhost), Web, 47.

9. Kelly D. Blessinger, "Problem Patrons: All Shapes and Sizes," *Reference Librarian* 36, no. 75/76 (2002): 3; Education Research Complete, Web, 47.

10. Since one campus occasionally enrolled students who were child prodigies and legally considered to be minors, age alone could not be the only factor used to determine the library's policy about who was a child.

11. This part of the policy was designed to deal with the requirements of both the Children's Internet Protection Act (CIPA) and the Children's Online Privacy Protection Act of 1998 (COPPA). Melissa A. Purcell, *The Networked Library: A Guide for the Educational Use of Social Networking Sites* (Santa Barbara, CA: Linworth, 2012); *eBook Collection* (EBSCOhost), Web, 28.

12. The Family Educational Rights and Privacy Act (FERPA) (20 U.S.C. § 1232g; 34 CFR Part 99) is a federal law that protects the privacy of students and which should be followed when revealing any information about library patrons. By inadvertently revealing who is in the library, the library staff could be helping a shooter identify a target; or by accidentally disclosing information about people working in the library, a library staff member could be creating an exploitable digital security weakness. Shuman, *Library Security and Safety Handbook: Prevention, Policies, and Procedures*, http://search.ebscohost.com/login .aspx?direct=true&scope=site&db=nlebk&db=nlabk&AN=45110, 223.

13. The National Incident Management System (NIMS) is an incident preparedness system implemented by the U.S. Department of Homeland Security.

14. Guy Robertson, "Flood Protection: Avoiding the Wrong Mixture," *Feliciter* 59, no. 4 (2013): 46–51; Education Research Complete, Web, 46.

15. Donna Hirst, "The Iowa City Flood of 2008: A Librarian and IT Professional's Perspective," *Information Technology & Libraries* 27, no. 4 (2008): 5–8; Education Research Complete, Web, 5.

GARY FITSIMMONS

10

Why Shared Governance Is Both the Worst and Best Model for Decision-Making in Academic Libraries

HAVING WORKED FOR BOTH GOOD and poor bosses in many different jobs, I have seen the need for shared governance (within certain limitations) in every industry or job situation, and libraries are no different in this respect. There is little worse for morale than the feeling of being trapped in a morass of inefficiency where one cannot even suggest simple improvements to make things better. When in such a situation, it is tempting to think, "If I were in charge, things would be different!" What one learns after being placed in charge is that many of the decisions to be made are not as cut and dried as previously perceived, and no matter what decision you make in many situations, you will not be able to please everyone. So what is the solution for the beleaguered leader? Enter shared governance to save the day! No, it won't always automatically make the best answer to every problem rise to the top or suddenly make everyone agree with you, but it will allow for possibly better solutions to be aired and for each member of your staff to feel that they have some say in the decisions that are made.

Shared governance in higher education was set forth in the 1966 "Statement on Government of Colleges and Universities" as the idea that "multiple members of the campus should have input on key decisions," such as "questions over general education policy, the framing and execution of long-range plans, budgeting, and presidential selection" (Kezar, 2002, 946). More specifically and more relevant to our discussion here, "It has historically retained the notion of the importance of consultation and participation of campus constituents in major decision-making, reflecting democratic principles" (Kezar, 2002, 946–47). Applying this more specific definition to library governance is as simple as substituting the word "library" for the word "campus," and recognizing that the idea of shared governance carries with it a certain amount of decentralization in the governance process and structure. Thus, governance may be seen as a continuum with a rigid top-down structure of decision-making at one end and an equally rigid democratic structure of decision-making at the other end. Each end has its advantages and disadvantages, with most academic libraries opting for a chance to have the best of both worlds by employing a model somewhere in between the two extremes. Let's first look at the general characteristics of each of the two major models.

THE TOP-DOWN MODEL

The top-down, purely hierarchical structure is the most centralized form, with all major decisions decreed by the library CEO. Extreme cases would even extend that centralized decision-making to smaller decisions, resulting in micromanagement, where individual displays of creativity are punished and the blind following of orders is rewarded. In our society, the disadvantages of such a structure seem obvious. It leads to low motivation, low levels of innovation, and low morale among staff members, and the manager will eventually wear himself out. I have seen (and pitied) library directors who cannot leave their library for any appreciable amount of time for fear that someone on the staff will do something wrong and the director will have to clean up the mess. If these directors do get away to a conference, they spend an inordinate amount of time on their cell phones and e-mail making sure things are being done "correctly" at "their" library. There are, however, advantages to the top-down model which should be noted. Decisions are more likely to be consistent, they are more quickly made since only one person is involved, and everyone often has a clearer idea of expectations.

THE PURELY DEMOCRATIC MODEL

On the other hand, a completely democratic structure dictates that all decisions are made by everyone as a group, by majority vote. The advantages are that everyone has an equal say in how the library is run, leading to better morale and theoretically to less stress on the director relative to decision-making. Unfortunately, decision-making using this structure can be divisive if there are equally strong opinions on two sides of an issue, and no give-and-take. The director may also actually feel more stress relative to a decision, since she will be held accountable for it even if it was not what she would have decided if making the decision alone.

Another interesting thing about this structure is that it seldom takes into account every constituency of the library, even just for major decisions, because of the major drawback of this model, which is a lack of agility in decision-making. It takes considerable time and effort to adequately inform and then poll even just a few people on just one issue, much more so all of the constituent users and supporters of an academic library for every major decision. This statement also begs the question of what parameters are used to define which decisions to be made are major decisions. Consequently, what usually happens if this model is in play is that an oligarchy (the library staff, or even just the librarians) makes the decisions by majority vote.

SHARED GOVERNANCE APPROACHES

This, of course, is at least a partially shared-governance approach, which gives those who are allowed to participate a say in how the library is run. Most academic libraries gravitate to something like this type of shared-governance approach (often using a representative structure in larger libraries), with those who are allowed to participate being those who actually care to do so. In such cases, the expediency of the need for agility in decision-making overcomes the desire for pure democracy and those who are most likely to care enough to cast a vote on major decisions are given the freedom to do so without the encumbrance of the apathy of the other library constituents. It is worth noting here that even those who usually don't care will care deeply about certain issues (not always predictably), and will feel left out or even betrayed when they are not consulted on these issues.

While the above approach has more flexibility than a totally democratic approach and offers equal say to the participants, it still requires enough consensus-building in order to get a clear majority. Far from a simple duality of possible positions on each decision, there are probably at least as many different ways to run any aspect of library services as there are people involved in doing so. It is not hard to envision the chaos that would ensue if all of these competing views of how to offer library services were forever being voted on with no clear winner. Hence the need for give-and-take consensus-building in establishing policy in every area. Some policies will, of necessity, be dictated from higher up in the institution. For everything else, there must be an agreed-upon outline of what decision-making power is allotted to each position for each function of that position, and the parameters for which types of decisions require conferring with others, and to what extent. Strong, well-thought-out policies in this regard will keep to a minimum the amount of renegotiation that must happen as boundaries are pressed to realign daily for the sake of making progress.

THE KEYS TO SHARED GOVERNANCE: LEADERSHIP AND CONSENSUS-BUILDING

As alluded to earlier, a completely democratic form of decision-making is non-existent in any academic library simply because of its impracticality. That is why there is almost always a CEO position over the library, even though in some cases that position is elected or rotates among the librarians. There will always come a point at one time or another when a final decision will have to be made with the authority to make it stick. In any library with a direc-tor position, that authority has already been delegated to the director (unless there is a dysfunctional situation where someone other than the director is actually running the library). With that assumption, let us next consider how a blended system of top-down and shared governance can make the deci-sion-making process work smoothly enough to keep everyone happy.

One of the most critical skills a library director must have is making proper use of shared governance to secure buy-in from stakeholders. With-out such support, you can kiss your chances of accomplishing anything of substance as a library director good-bye. With such support, nearly anything (within reason) is possible. In terms of securing buy-in from staff, no other model for decision-making comes close to shared governance for a variety of reasons. But shared governance can also be fraught with perils for the unini-tiated and for the thoughtless leader. It also takes much more work initially than simply issuing edicts to be obeyed, but the savings in effort occurs on the action side once the decision has been made.

POLICIES FOR PARAMETERS AND PROCESS

It is important at this point to understand that blending shared governance with top-down leadership necessitates an understanding of both the parame-ters and the process by which decisions must be made. It means that, first of all, the CEO of the library has the final and ultimate authority in making deci-sions about the library, subject, of course, to the limitations imposed on him by the institution and his superiors. Secondly, along with that authority comes the responsibility to consult with the stakeholders relative to each decision. Whoever is realistically affected in any significant degree (library staff, staff in other departments, faculty, students, the community, alumni, etc.) should be at least consulted before a final decision is made. Given this, it shouldn't be too hard to see that the main disadvantages of using shared governance in making decisions is the excessive time and effort needed to do it well. When deadlines are approaching, expectations are rising, and pressure is mounting, it is tempting for the director to short-circuit the shared governance process, either by using it only for really major decisions or by limiting participation to those with whom the director happens to have current easy access. As in an electrical circuit, a short is a dangerous situation that can cause damage to the whole system, so short-circuiting the shared governance process damages the relationships in the system, causing mistrust, which will render the library less effective in carrying out its mission.

Clearly, to make the process work smoothly and to stave off any emergency situations that might seem to call for short-circuiting the process, there is a need for well-thought-out policies and parameters to keep the process going in the right direction. This starts at the grassroots level with good job descriptions, laying out the expectations and parameters of each position. Interaction between positions is dictated by policies relating to every function covered in providing library services. These should include a listing of each position or constituency involved in each type of decision, the means of mediation when there is disagreement, the appropriate consequences if policy is not followed, and the means of amending policy to cover unforeseen circumstances. When such a system is solidly in place and being followed, the library director is much freer to form a vision and think ahead rather than spending all of his time putting out fires. This forming of the vision is also in turn a major factor in encouraging the contributions of each member, which keeps the system oiled and running smoothly.

Unfortunately, setting up such policies is not an easy task. Most library policy manuals range from outdated to nonexistent. But, more positively, a library director can usually enlist the help of her staff in rectifying this situation by having them update their own job descriptions and work together to update policies about each of their areas of involvement. As each policy is updated into rough draft form, it can then be passed by the entire group for input. With the final approval of the director, the policy manual should be submitted for approval by the administration of the institution in order to avoid potential conflicts down the road. (A more complete rendering of this process is given in the series of articles by Fitsimmons, 2011–12a-c.) Note that updating and formulating new policies are an ongoing process that must be conducted continuously as a matter of course while providing regular library services.

Having learned how to work with your staff in formulating and updating policies will then place you in the position to work with them in enforcing those policies. Although having good policies is critical to the smooth operation of any library, you must understand that as a manager, your job is more than just enforcing policies. A machine can do that by following its programming. A good manager discerns the delicate distinctions in circumstances that will never be fully covered by any policy and knows how to treat each situation as called for by those differing circumstances. He then trains the staff in how to deal with such occasions in their areas of responsibility. Sometimes that will call for updating policy, but more often than not it will call for dealing with situations on a case-by-case basis, without ignoring set policy. Here is where shared governance on a microscale can be invaluable. By consulting with those directly involved in a specific circumstance, you can put your heads together and come up with great solutions to many sticky situations while winning the trust of those concerned. It's a win-win proposition when it is done consistently across the board, time after time. Once you have trained your staff to employ this process, you can delegate many decision-making situations to them, acting as more of a facilitator, and stepping into the process only when absolutely necessary.

INTEGRITY MAKES IT WORK

Now having said all of this, you must realize that you will run into situations where it doesn't seem possible to please anyone, much less everyone. These are the times when you must be able to rely on the goodwill that you have won with all of the careful sharing of governance that you have done up to that point. Shared governance is a great tool for gaining buy-in, but it can never replace your own integrity. If a choice must be made between gaining buy-in and doing the right thing, always do the right thing. But the point of using shared governance is to gain buy-in to support you in doing the right thing. Often the process of consulting brings the clarity necessary to discern the right thing to do. Integrity breeds trust, and that trust is worth more than having absolute authority in any matter because it is the key to implementing decisions and plans in the future.

Finally, always remember the importance of operating with the utmost consistency under the shared governance model that you have worked out together. If your staff point out your inconsistencies in applying policies or employing the process as laid out in the policies, do not consider it disrespect or disregard for your authority. Instead, remember that they have a stake in things running smoothly just as you do and see them as contributing to that goal. Acknowledge your need for improvement and move on, just as you would hope that they acknowledge their need for improvement when they are corrected. A good dose of humility, especially being modeled by the director, is required to do shared governance well.

In my experience, although the approach I have described here takes a lot of work and constant vigilance to make sure one is continuing to lead in integrity with all affected parties, it saves a lot of trouble down the road. Many times I have been grateful that I shared the decision-making with my staff and sought input from faculty, students, and other constituencies because they have come up with better solutions to the problems under consideration than my false dichotomies would allow. It is also a great morale-builder for people to see that their good ideas are being heard and acted upon. Unfortunately, the library director must occasionally decide against even a majority, because of inside knowledge that is sensitive (such as personnel issues) and cannot be divulged. In these situations, people will be much more understanding and able to give you the benefit of a doubt if you have not built up a reputation for being capricious or arbitrary.

CONCLUSION

In conclusion, note the reasons that shared governance, if done poorly, is the worst possible model for decision-making in an academic library: lack of clarity, slowness, and a tremendous amount of work required for decision-making. On the other hand, note the reasons that shared governance done well is the best possible model for decision-making in an academic library: better thought-out decisions that genuinely address real problems, resulting in high morale and satisfaction among affected constituencies, with fewer policy compliance issues or other negative reactions to decisions that are made. For the director and her results-oriented boss, the time and effort needed to do shared governance well are not only worth their while, but are critical investments to make.

REFERENCES

Fitsimmons, Gary. 2011. "The Policy/Procedure Manual Part I: Making and Abiding by Good Policies." *The Bottom Line: Managing Library Finances* 24, no. 4: 233–35.

———. 2012a. "The Policy/Procedure Manual Part II: Procedures That Complement Good Policies." *The Bottom Line: Managing Library Finances* 25, no. 1: 13–15.

———. 2012b. "The Policy/Procedure Manual Part III: Organizing the Manual." *The Bottom Line: Managing Library Finances* 25, no. 2: 56–59.

———. 2012c. "The Policy/Procedure Manual Part IV: Writing the Manual." *The Bottom Line: Managing Library Finances* 25, no. 3: 95–97.

Kezar, Adrianna. 2002. "Governance and Decision-Making in Colleges and Universities." In *Encyclopedia of Education,* edited by James W. Guthrie, vol. 3: 945–49. 2nd edition. New York: Macmillan Reference USA; *Gale Virtual Reference Library,* Web.

PATRICIA TULLY

11
Relationships with Stakeholders

ON AUGUST 26, 2014, I was dismissed from my position as Wesleyan University (Connecticut) librarian after a series of escalating disagreements with my supervisor Ruth Weissman, then Wesleyan's provost and vice president for academic affairs. My open letter to Wesleyan's faculty describing the circumstances surrounding the firing became public in a post on the student blog, *Wesleying,* and an article in *Inside Higher Ed.* Since then, I have been reflecting on the months before the firing. How did my actions and reactions affect my working relationship with the provost, and could I have changed the outcome if I had acted differently?

HIGHER EDUCATION IS CHANGING

It is a truism that libraries—along with higher education and all other aspects of life—are undergoing radical changes as a result of emerging technologies. The Wesleyan University Library's mission "is to provide the information services and resources required to support the learning, teaching and research of the Wesleyan community." The mission remains the same, but the scholarship and research that must be supported—and the systems to disseminate them—are undergoing a revolution. Technology is changing how students, scholars, and researchers find information, how they use and manipulate that information, and their expectations for accessing it. And the revolution continues with the development and diversification of technological devices and systems, and subsequent changes in academic work and communication. Seizing the opportunities and responding to the challenges of these changes takes commitment—of thought, time, and money. And this is in an academic environment that does not have increased staffing or funding to support a much richer, but more complex and expensive, scholarly landscape.

LIBRARIES ARE CHANGING

Academic libraries must continue to support teaching, learning, and scholarship in this revolutionary time. More information and resources are available in a variety of electronic formats, but in many disciplines print books and other materials are still important. When libraries are doing their job well, the complex work of negotiating access, providing search mechanisms to find and use needed information, and troubleshooting problems is all but invisible. And the invisibility of the work makes it difficult for those outside the library to understand its complexity and cost. In such an environment, library administrators must effectively make the case to senior campus leadership to support library initiatives and ongoing operations. Making the case is sometimes made more difficult by an artifact of a bygone era—the librarian stereotype. Bun, glasses, dedicated to print, buried in the past, irrelevant in today's technological world. I don't know a single librarian who fits this stereotype. But in dealing with some faculty members and campus administrators, the stereotype makes it hard for them to hear what we have to say. Instead, a common assumption (made more attractive by the many competing demands on university budgets and staffing) is that technology has made library services mostly unnecessary and redundant. In the minds of many campus administrators, libraries are the buggy-whip factories of the twenty-first century.

THE SITUATION AT WESLEYAN

In 2009 a decision was made by senior campus administrators to move the Art Library from the Center for the Arts area of campus into Olin, the main campus library. The Art Library was in a small building that lacked air conditioning and had been out of shelf space for twenty years. As a result, half of the art collection had been transferred to Olin by 2010. However, the Art Library was near the Art & Art History Department's faculty offices and classrooms, and it was part of an award-winning complex of buildings that constitute the Center for the Arts at Wesleyan. Students loved the coziness and quiet of the Art Library, and faculty loved the knowledgeable, service-oriented staff and the convenience of stopping in before class to pick up materials. But the space was inadequate and not conducive for the long-term preservation of the collection. Something needed to be done.

I found out that a decision had been made to move the Art Library in a 2010 meeting with students from the Academic Affairs Committee of the Wesleyan Student Assembly. I met with them periodically to talk about student ideas for improving the library, and to review with them new library initiatives. A student mentioned in passing that in a meeting with the president they were told that the Art Library was moving into Olin that summer. I told them truthfully that this was the first I had heard of it and I would respond after speaking with the provost.

After the meeting I contacted then-Provost Joseph Bruno. He confirmed that the Art Library would be moving into Olin. I said that in order to do this, the library would need to undertake a major weeding of the collections. Olin was almost out of space, despite the recent weeding of additional copies, print volumes of journals available online, and the installation of compact shelving. The proposed weeding project, therefore, would have to consider the withdrawal of certain last copies of books in the collection—books that would be available through interlibrary loan from other libraries, but would no longer be on Wesleyan's shelves. This would be unpopular with many members of Wesleyan's faculty, who supported the library but were against withdrawing any last copies. A last-copy weeding project had not been done in at least fifty years at Wesleyan. This project would take longer to complete than the few months before the summer, and the provost approved a delay in the move while we conducted a three-year weeding project.

As the project proceeded, the administration worked with Art & Art History to overcome student and faculty opposition to the move of the Art Library. New faculty offices for Art & Art History were created in a renovated building nearer the center of campus, and the Office of Academic Affairs and the library worked closely with faculty on the requirements of an art space within Olin Library. The location of the new space remained an issue, however. The Center for the Arts had been created in the 1970s as the arts space on Wesleyan's campus, and moving the Art Library out of that space was eroding the reality of a central space for the arts at Wesleyan. Students continued to object to the loss of the Art Library as a quiet study and research space.

When Ruth Weissman became provost in July 2013, one of her first actions was to give priority to the planning and implementation of the Art Library move by the following summer. And she did so—putting Senior

Associate Provost Karen Anderson and Arts and Humanities Dean Andrew Curran in charge of the project. The library worked closely with them and with campus Construction Services to design new art study spaces within Olin that were attractive and functional: the resulting design delighted the faculty and helped students to come to terms with the loss of the old Art Library. In the summer of 2014 the weeding project came to an end with a major shift of the collections to make room for the incoming art collection of 50,000 volumes, and Olin spaces were renovated. By the end of the summer of 2014, both projects were complete and completely successful.

And by the end of that summer, I was no longer Wesleyan University librarian—dismissed, effective immediately, by the provost with no cause cited. There was nothing actionable in this—mine was an "at-will" appointment, and could be ended without cause by either party. What happened?

WHAT I DID RIGHT

As university librarian, I led several projects and initiatives that can be minefields for academic library leaders. On becoming university librarian in 2009, we were faced with the loss of six library positions due to university staffing cuts through an early retirement program. The resulting adjustments in all three university libraries affected every library position in some way, and many of these changes were difficult. I worked closely with librarians and library staff, the provost, and divisional deans to phase in the changes over a period of six months, while minimizing the adverse effects on library services. I listened to everyone who was affected—I understood their anger and worry, their feeling of loss, and I listened to their ideas and suggestions for changes. And all this, although it took patience and time, led to a successful, sustainable new organization. We were even able to implement improvements in the library liaison program with academic departments, and in consolidating some library functions.

The weeding project and move of the Art Library were also challenging. But the same collaborative, transparent style that worked in reorganizing the library proved effective in leading these initiatives. When the weeding project began in the fall of 2011, faculty were outraged at the extent and scope of the project, so much so that we suspended it for a semester while we reviewed the project with faculty. We spoke to concerned faculty members individually, in department meetings, and in faculty meetings. We created and maintained a project blog that detailed the background, planning, and implementation of the project. And we made changes in the project to address as many faculty concerns as possible. At the end of the three-month suspension we resumed the project and completed it by the end of July 2014. Were all faculty members convinced by us of the project's value or advisability? By no means; I doubt that we changed many people's minds. But our openness and evident willingness to listen and make adjustments did maintain positive relationships with the faculty, as a group and as individuals. They knew that we heard their concerns and took them seriously, even if we did not always respond in the way they would have liked.

The move of the Art Library was particularly of concern to students majoring in Art & Art History, and they began a "Save the Art Library" movement. Although the decision to move the Art Library had been made, we listened to students' concerns about the move and the creation of art spaces within Olin. We attended protest meetings, and asked students what they wanted in new study spaces. The most effective method of doing this was low-tech—a whiteboard with Post-it notes in the Art and Olin libraries with questions—what do you like about the library? What don't you like? What improvements would you like to see? What is most important in a new art space in Olin? The resulting comments and discussions were enormously helpful as the design of the new space took shape in the fall of 2013.

With library staff, with faculty, and with students I maintained an open, transparent, nonjudgmental leadership style that made people feel heard and valued, and encouraged them to be honest in expressing their concerns and their ideas for producing the best possible result for the library and our ability to support the work of students and faculty. Even the most controversial and emotionally fraught projects—and all three of the projects described above were both—were successful while maintaining positive, effective working relationships between the library and other constituencies on campus.

WHAT I DID WRONG

If I did so well, why was I fired? Although I was given no reason for the dismissal, I was less than proud of some of my actions and reactions in the months preceding it.

As I mentioned above, Wesleyan's administration sometimes made decisions without consulting with affected departments, or notifying them that a decision had been made. This was not always the case, but when it happened it was galling to me. And I let it be known to the provost and other university administrators that I was angry about the lack of transparency and perceived lack of respect for myself as university librarian and for the library in general. As the number of instances grew, my anger increased and with it my expression of that anger. I was silent and gloomy in meetings and participated less than I should have in discussions of the many positive projects and initiatives going on at the university. In short, I sulked.

My predecessor, Barbara Jones, had been invited to attend weekly meetings between the provost and the academic deans, and on becoming university librarian I attended these meetings as well. It was useful to hear about curricular changes and other challenges facing Academic Affairs—although I rarely spoke in meetings, I was often able to take back information to the library that we used to improve services and access to resources. When Ruth Weissman became provost in July 2013, I was no longer invited to attend the meetings. When I objected, the provost said they were not a good use of my time. I felt cut off from Academic Affairs—my connection was reduced to a monthly meeting with the provost. I continued to push for regular meetings with the deans, either individually or as a group. Instead, after several months, the provost invited me and two other librarians to monthly faculty luncheon talks as her guests. I did not attend these lunches, instead recommending three librarians to attend who I thought would most benefit from them. My stated reason for not accepting the provost's invitation was a plausible one—it was useful for other librarians to learn about faculty research. But I also felt that the invitation was a sop to mollify me with regard to the diminution of my role in Academic Affairs, and I was determined not to accept it.

At the beginning of Professor Weissman's term as provost, she called a meeting to begin the planning of the move of the Art Library and was very specific about how she expected the planning to proceed. I said that I would organize the planning as she instructed. But I decided that her directions would not be the most effective way to develop or implement the plan. At the next meeting of the group, I described what I had done and why I felt a different approach would be better. I suggested that the provost give us a deadline and desired outcomes and let the group develop a plan for getting there. The provost was not pleased, and the Arts & Humanities dean was assigned to develop the plan according to the provost's direction. I realized that the setting and timing of my proposal were all wrong; I should have made my counterproposal directly to the provost and in a private meeting with her. I was in effect calling her out at a time when she was just beginning to establish herself in her new position.

In my interactions with colleagues, library staff, staff in other departments, and community partners, I try to be fair, open, and positive. I value people's differences and how those differences enhance the work we do together. I might feel annoyed, worried, or overwhelmed at times, but I strive not to let those feelings affect the work or the relationship. But I was not always as forbearing toward senior administrators at Wesleyan, or as careful to grow and maintain positive working relationships with them. I believe I had reason to be angry about the lack of transparency and consultation about initiatives that affected the library. However, my actions in response fed the dysfunctional relationship and did not benefit the library. I did not keep my eyes on the prize—that of keeping the library a partner in campus discussions and initiatives.

I would not recommend to anyone that they continue in a situation in which they feel disrespected and unheard—and that is the situation I ultimately found myself in at Wesleyan. What should I have done instead? The prudent course would have been to maintain a professional demeanor while looking for other job opportunities. Once established in a new position, I could have pointed out my concerns about administrative practices at Wesleyan, and how they have hindered the accomplishment of the university's liberal arts mission. I did not take this course because I love so much about Wesleyan and the surrounding community—and because I let my anger take over. The campus discussion following my public dismissal led to some beneficial changes at Wesleyan. There is a great deal of satisfaction in that. If I had controlled my anger while remaining a strong advocate for the library, I might still have been dismissed. But it would have kept open the possibility of communication between the library and senior administrators, and that is always beneficial no matter what the ultimate outcome.

■ ■ ■

MOVING ON

In February 2015 I took a yearlong interim position as Assistant Director at Russell Library, Middletown's public library. I learned about a different kind of librarianship there from a director and staff who are smart, compassionate, and dedicated to serving the whole of Middletown's diverse community. While job hunting I remained active in community organizations, and it was with mixed emotions that I accepted a position as Director of the Ketchikan (Alaska) Public Library in early 2017. Ketchikan has welcomed me with open arms, and I am proud to be a member of this beautiful and vibrant community.

My time after Wesleyan was a period of intense growth and change. Looking back, I am content with my actions after my appointment was terminated, while being committed to not making the same mistakes that led to my termination.

ADAM MURRAY

12
Reframing Community Relations

Four Perspectives on a Children's Book Event

EACH YEAR A MIDSIZED, regional, comprehensive university library system hosts an event in which 200 regional public schoolchildren select 2,000 children's books for their school library/media centers. Giving the books away serves as the core of an event—named the Book Bonanza—around which a variety of on- and off-campus partners unite to nurture community relations. The development of this event from an idea into a reality offered many lessons for me as a library dean on the nature of community relations and engagement. This critical reflection utilizes Bolman and Deal's four frames of organizations to examine lessons that are important for library leaders to consider when working on community relations projects and initiatives (Bolman and Deal, 2013).

Institutions of higher education in America have a long and rich history of involvement with the communities in which they are situated. Increasingly, colleges and universities are looked to for workforce development, economic development, cultural engagement, and locally relevant research in addition to their role of preparing students for success in a global society. University presidents, provosts, and deans are expected to balance these expectations, developing creative ways of fostering positive community relationships while maintaining higher education's core mission of teaching, learning, and research. Community relationships have long-term impacts on recruitment efforts, which is yet another area where deans—including library deans—are expected to contribute (Hubbard and Loos, 2013, 173).

Bolman and Deal (2013) have proposed four different frames or perspectives through which any leadership position or situation should be viewed. These four frames are the structural frame, the human resources frame, the political frame, and the symbolic frame, or more simply the factory, the family, the jungle, and the temple respectively. They state that any given leadership situation can be examined through these different frames in order to reveal a clearer context for decision-making. While any given situation may have elements that fall more clearly within one or two frames than equally within all four, there are usually elements of each that should be considered in a leadership role. Below are brief overviews of the four frames.

Structural: As its name implies, this frame focuses on the structures that make up an organization, and are often thought of as synonymous with the organization itself. Artifacts of the structural frame are the organization chart, policies and procedures, workflows, and other formally defined elements of the organization that are assumed to operate independently of the people employed by the organization.

Human resources: This frame, also simply called "the family," represents not just the people who are involved in and employed by an organization, but also how those employees are treated. Promotion and disciplinary actions, support for professional development, and the creation and sustaining of workplace practices that empower employees are all examples of the human resources frame.

Political: Bolman and Deal discuss the notion that politics is simply the result of scarce resources in the context of competing needs or differences of opinion. In this perspective, the political frame is a reality of organizational leadership, but it does not have the negative connotation traditionally associated with the word *politics.* The influence or power possessed or exerted by an organization, its leaders, and its employees are artifacts of the political frame.

Symbolic: The final frame stands in a dichotomous relationship with the structural frame. The structural frame is highly logical and objective, whereas the symbolic frame recognizes the emotional context of a workplace. In this perspective, the leader serves not only as an organizational architect, but he or she also serves in a role that can best be described as a "priest" or "prophet." Myths that exemplify organizational culture or history, logos, and vision/value statements are artifacts of this frame.

This chapter uses these four frames to examine an academic library's initiation of and participation in a community relations and engagement event named the Book Bonanza.

THE STRUCTURAL FRAME OF THE BOOK BONANZA

Once the idea of the Book Bonanza was pitched to the relevant offices on campus (discussed in the "Political Frame" section below) and these offices were on board with the concept of the event, the difficult work of planning the event began. One of the first steps in this was finalizing the intended audience and determining a date that would work not only with the facilities available on campus that could accommodate the projected crowd, but would work with the school districts' calendars. The event had, at its core, the distribution of children's books to school districts within the university's service region. These books were for all ages, so the intended participants ranged from kindergartners to high school students. Given the differences between the academic years in a university and surrounding school systems, this was a problematic task when also considering the testing schedules mandated by the state for students of different grades. Identifying with whom to work to schedule and coordinate the event in the school districts was also an initial step required in order to begin planning.

Once a suitable date was discovered and the location on campus was secured, the project turned toward internal and external logistics. External logistics included distributing formal invitations to the event which communicated the purpose of the event, its intended participants, and the number of children (plus chaperones) to be invited to the event. Some school districts needed to get approval from the superintendent, requiring specific paperwork or information related to liability, and transportation had to be arranged. Information about food allergies and accommodations for children with disabilities needed to be gathered and incorporated into the planning for internal logistics.

The internal logistics were even more complicated. The event was to be hosted in a large ballroom in the university's student center, some distance away from where the children's books were stored in the university's library. Not only did the planning process need to accommodate the transport of the books to the event location, it also needed to accommodate the packing of the books selected by the children into boxes to be loaded on the buses for their return trip. The books needed to be organized by age/reading level so that children of different ages could be directed to the appropriate tables. This also influenced the layout of the room, in order to best facilitate the flow of children around the event. Given the geographic distances of some participating school districts from the university, buses from different districts had different arrival times, requiring the development of a program of activities for the earlier arrivals. Likewise, geographic distance determined the departure times for buses to return to the schools in a manner that allowed the children to be on time for buses home or after-school pickup. These geographic issues influenced the development of a schedule for the children to pick the books for their district, along with the lunch schedule. One unforeseen difficulty encountered in developing the schedule was that schoolchildren have lunch on a very different schedule than at a university, with some children hungry by mid-morning.

Other structural issues related to internal logistics included scheduling the university president, arranging for giveaways for the children, coordinating with media outlets, and arranging supplies for the event.

THE HUMAN RESOURCES FRAME OF THE BOOK BONANZA

Given that most academic libraries do not employ someone specifically responsible for community relations or event planning, the development and implementation of this event required a well-deliberated approach to the human resources needed to successfully carry out the event.

A planning team was assembled of library faculty and staff who had expertise and/or responsibility in areas needed for the event. This team included the library's marketing coordinator, gifts coordinator, budget officer, education librarian, director of technical services, executive assistant to the dean, and the dean. In addition, this team included other university partners who helped fund and coordinate the event, including the director of enrollment management, the associate director of enrollment management responsible for campus tours, the Town & Gown director, and the director of regional outreach.

Specific tasks that fell to library employees included booking the event location, managing RSVP information from the schools (including food allergies and accommodations), sorting and transporting the books, writing press releases, and purchasing and assembling gift bags for the children. As the dean, I undertook requests to University Athletics for the presence of the university's mascot, scheduling the president to speak briefly at the event, and working with the president's office to reimburse the school districts for their travel expenses.

Because some of these activities fell outside of the normal day-to-day work of the library employees, the members of the planning team needed to be clear on who was taking the lead on each item. A planning document was created using Google Docs and shared with each member of the planning team, allowing the team to monitor the status of the various projects required. In addition, these members needed to discuss where the coordination of this event fell in their existing load of responsibility, in order to appropriately balance their normal activities with work associated with the event.

THE POLITICAL FRAME OF THE BOOK BONANZA

While the previous two frames involved many members of the library, the political frame fell heavily on me as the dean. Other than providing some guidance on overall goals or approval on expenditures for the event, I left much of the structural- and human resource-related items to the planning team and their supervisors to address. The political elements of the Book Bonanza can be roughly sorted into two categories: pitching the event, and assembling a coalition of allies to make the event successful.

The foundation for pitching the event rested with a presidential mandate for all units on campus to actively contribute to recruitment events. This mandate, issued early in the fiscal year by our interim president, was communicated consistently in his messages and speeches. Based on this expectation for all units to be involved in enrollment, the library leadership team conceived of a method of distributing a large number of children's books that had been given to the library. This stockpile, which didn't meet the collection profile of the library or of the College of Education's Media Resources Center, occupied a large amount of storage space. A number of different methods for disposing of the collection had been considered, including a children's book sale, but ultimately we settled on the concept of giving the books to the school media centers in our university's service region. This became an enrollment initiative when we decided that we would bring children to campus to select the books, giving them opportunities to see university life. In addition to selected books for their school media centers, the invited children would also have an opportunity to pick out a book for themselves.

With this concept in mind, I began working with leaders on campus who could help put together such an event. Because the university maintained an active Town & Gown partnership program, and because I served on the advisory board for the Town & Gown program, I first approached this program's director. With his support, we brainstormed other units on campus that would be interested and essential in helping with the event. Once the leadership within enrollment management and regional outreach were on board, we were able to start making the event a reality.

As planning began, it became obvious that resources beyond that of the library would be needed to make the event successful and memorable for the children involved. This involved pitching the event beyond the coalition of offices helping to plan the event. I scheduled time with the president in order to discuss funding for reimbursing the school systems for transportation charges incurred by participation, as well as welcoming the children and chaperones to campus. Likewise, after the planning team was unable to schedule the presence of the university's athletic mascot, I met with the director of athletics to describe the event and how it fit within the president's recruitment mandate. Both pitches were successful.

The final and most difficult pitch was to the university's Media Relations Department. Because this type of event was not normal for the library to put on, the Media Relations Department did not initially understand either the implications of the event as a recruitment effort or the community goodwill that the event would generate. They also wanted to attribute the event to Town & Gown or the Office of Regional Outreach, since they were more accustomed to these offices putting on such events. It ultimately required an e-mail of explanation and encouragement from the president to the Media Relations Department to finalize their willingness to coordinate local TV and newspaper coverage, and to give the library appropriate prominence in the coverage.

THE SYMBOLIC FRAME
OF THE BOOK BONANZA

As described earlier, the symbolic frame focuses on the emotional and personal connections people feel towards a situation or institution. The frame recognizes the illogical and emotional responses that people naturally have toward organizations or the actions they take. Recognition of the emotional impact of the Book Bonanza event was important to keep in mind from the outset.

The children who participated in the event would not differentiate between the library that sponsored the event and the university they visited. Creating a signature moment during which an emotional connection to the institution could be shaped is the very essence of a recruitment effort. We received an outpouring of gratitude from the children and the parents who served as chaperones for the event. We also received overwhelming positivity from the school media center coordinators, who established a closer connection to the dean of the College of Education (who was also invited to the event) and the education librarian. While the event was conceptualized as a recruitment event for the children in an undergraduate capacity, an unforeseen consequence was the possibility of recruiting the teachers who attended the event into further credentialing or graduate programs offered by the College of Education.

The messaging that accompanied the event likewise had an important symbolic role. This messaging consisted of two key elements. The first of these was reiterating that the university gives back to the community in which it is housed. The second was focused on the role of literacy as a pathway to higher education and lifelong learning, with the academic library standing as a partner in these efforts, rather than serving simply as a facility for books and computers.

CLOSING REFLECTIONS

In reflecting on the Book Bonanza event, and on the role of academic libraries in recruitment efforts and community relationships at institutions of higher education in general, I was struck by the overwhelming goodwill that conceiving and hosting this event provided to the library. The image of the university library as a partner in community engagement and recruitment resonated throughout the university community, and was included in presidential highlights with the Board of Regents.

Every institution has its own recruitment strategies, but there are none better than an effort to engage children in a manner that also provides an opportunity for the university to give back to the community. The role of library administrators in responding to the needs of their institutions in such areas as recruitment requires them to think outside of the walls (virtual or physical) of the library, and to think creatively about how the library can leverage its available resources or services in order to create an opportunity that is a positive experience on many different fronts.

At the time that this event was planned, I was not yet familiar with Bolman and Deal's four frames. Since reading their work, I have come to recognize the value of using these frames to think through major leadership decisions, beyond those of this event. Using the four frames offers a valuable opportunity for leaders to act mindfully, creating the best chance of making successful decisions.

The work that was involved with planning the first year of the event was daunting, but it served to make the second year of the Book Bonanza even smoother. Meanwhile, word about the event spread among the university's service region, with many school districts expressing their eagerness to be invited back. When the university president spoke briefly at the event about his favorite book, Dr. Seuss's *Oh, the Places You Will Go,* we had no idea that later that day, a young girl would find that book and keep it as her gift from the university. When she proudly posed for a picture with the president, holding her new book, it was clear that we had succeeded not simply in building a library recruitment event that also fostered positive community relations, but that we had impacted 200 children's interest in reading in a profound and memorable way.

REFERENCES

Bolman, Lee, and Terrance Deal. 2013. *Reframing Organizations: Artistry, Choice, & Leadership* 5th edition. San Francisco: Jossey-Bass.

Hubbard, Melissa, and Amber Loos. 2013. "Academic Library Participation in Recruitment and Retention Initiatives." *Reference Services Review* 41: 157–81.

CHRISTOPHER SHAFFER

13

Cultural Diversity Programming at Academic Libraries

Skills for Success

PROGRAMMING IS AN EXCELLENT way for an academic library to increase its visibility among members of the university community that it serves, as well as the community at large in which the university exists. As M. Kathleen Kern (2014, 210) notes in a recent article, "programming is becoming a burgeoning area of user services and can be a great way to connect people to the materials your library has on a particular subject." By hosting unique programs that appeal to a wide variety of individuals, library deans and directors can encourage students to come to the library who might not typically visit unless they absolutely must do so because of a research project. Programming that is open to the public at large can also have a positive impact on how not just the library, but how the overall university is perceived within the community in which it operates. Furthermore, by attracting individuals from the community to the library through programming, the campus itself will be seen by people who might otherwise have never considered visiting it. In this way, it is possible that library programming could impact student recruitment to some degree.

Through chance, I developed an interest in library programming about seven years ago. At that point in my career I had written two small grants related to collection development, when I learned about the Tournees Film Festival. Tournees is a grant-funded French film festival that is administered by the French American Cultural Alliance and is geared toward universities in the United States. I knew that many students wanted more multicultural events on our campus, and I have always enjoyed international films. As with many of the programming projects I have been involved in, not only did I think the community I served would benefit, but I felt a personal reward because I was engaged with the topic.

Before beginning, it is important for the reader to understand some basics about my background. I am a moderate liberal. Most of the events that are discussed in this chapter occurred on the extension campus of a very conservative university in southeast Alabama. The population that campus draws from is (in general) very religious (Protestant), very conservative (guns are good, abortion is bad), and judging from where the dial is tuned on every public access television, they generally are consumers of Fox News. With all of this said, the reader should not think that I view the people living in this area with disdain, but rather the opposite. They are good people who are products of their environment and their own personal histories. To me, the role of a programming librarian is not to convert people to a different set of beliefs, but to expose the public to a variety of different perspectives, with which they can do as they choose. I believe this is key to successful diversity programming, because if the goal is to tell the audience that they are wrong in their beliefs and the way they live their lives, then that audience will naturally either tune out or walk out.

CREATIVITY, OPENNESS, CURIOSITY

A library's program should be as diverse as the population it serves in terms of culture, ethnicity, religion, and any variety of interests that relate back to the patron base. A librarian who keeps up with a variety of forms of media—newspapers, magazines, blogs, and the evening news—will be well-poised to find speakers and events that will be a good fit for potential programming. Frequently, I have had people ask me how I found out about a speaker we were hosting, and the answer was quite simple. I read about the person in the morning newspaper, and thought his story was compelling enough to host him for a lecture.

Lectures and events at our library have been remarkably diverse in nature, but not particularly controversial as a rule. We have hosted a Holocaust survivor, an expert on black cowboys, a prison reformer, a variety of authors, a filmmaker and his subject, a French film festival, an international film festival (some of these were potentially controversial in rural south Alabama, but pleasantly there were never any complaints), a wide variety of exhibits, and two teacher workshops. The only lecture that ever had me particularly nervous was when a group asked if I would host a speaker named Michael Schermer. I did not know anything about the group, but I researched Mr. Schermer online and found nothing that was controversial to me. Later I mentioned the group to my archivist, who said, "Do you realize you just invited the atheists to your conservative Alabama college?" There was little I could do but move forward. I did not want to censor the speaker, so I braced for the criticism that I was sure would follow. Amazingly, there was none. The attendance—138 people came—was excellent. Several of those in the audience were fervently Christian, but they listened to what Schermer had to say, and then asked questions in a respectful manner. In the end it was a huge success, and one that I would not have likely had if I had understood what the true topic was about. This final thought is a good segue for our next skill set.

KNOW YOUR COMMUNITY

Programming is an excellent opportunity for libraries to bring back to the brick-and-mortar building those patrons who now feel they only need the Internet. It is also a way to offer "a wide range of scholarly activities . . . to enable knowledge transfer among researchers, students and the public community, including seminars, book launches, panel discussions and conferences" (Leong, 2013, 220–21). My beliefs and core values do not match the community I serve. I would not be surprised if that were the case for many other librarians across the nation. I would be lying if I denied having a hidden agenda of wanting to educate and enlighten our patrons by introducing them to new ideas. However, I believe it is important to try to avoid offending or insulting a patron base. Instead, I prefer the idea of pushing the envelope, and exposing patrons to a variety of ideas in a nonthreatening manner. Plus, if I think something would be incredibly controversial, more likely than not I would avoid that topic and move on to something else. It is worth noting that sometimes people can be surprising, and positively so. Had I known that an atheist group was requesting to use the library to host a speaker, I probably would have turned them down. In so doing, a great lecture and opportunity for dialogue would have been missed. No one changed their beliefs because of this event (nor should they have), but I have always thought that both sides understood each other's points of view far better at the end of the lecture than they did at the beginning.

Another example of knowing the community served came into play in 2014, when our library hosted a year of programming related to Islam. This was a result of a successful series of grants relating to the National Endowment for the Arts' *Muslim Journeys* initiative. As a result of the 9/11 attacks, U.S. involvement in the Middle East, and various other terrorist incidents over the past several years, there is a combination of prejudice, fear, and curiosity surrounding the Muslim community. Curiosity was the opening for successful programming. People in the community wanted to understand this group of people that was so remarkably foreign to them. They wanted to learn about their history, their past relations with not just the United States, but with the West in general, and because the various conflicts relating to Muslims went back to religion, they wanted to understand the Islamic faith.

All of these factors led to my developing an interfaith series of discussions surrounding the *Muslim Journeys* series of books. Partnerships were formed with the local Presbyterian church, the local Jewish temple, and the mosque. Religious leaders from these institutions led the first book discussion. Afterwards, book discussions were led by faculty members from our university. Attendance was strong because of the interfaith angle. Attendees were particularly interested in learning about the numerous similarities between their faith and Islam. Ultimately, the events were successful because they were nonthreatening, they promoted education and understanding, and there was a natural pool of attendees stemming from the partnerships with area religious institutions. The events also "stressed commonalities across groups rather than differences," which helped make them accessible to all in attendance (Hanna, Cooper, and Crumrin, 2011, 112).

EVENT PLANNING AND PROMOTION

Event planning and promotion are critical to the success of multicultural programming. The best program in the world is useless if no one is in attendance. It should be possible for a librarian to determine reasonably quickly what days/nights and times are best for maximum attendance. In my case, I discovered that planning events for Tuesday nights and Sunday afternoons led to the best attendance figures for the population that I served.

I approach promotion from a number of angles. Posters about the library's events are displayed not only on campus, but also at businesses patronized by people who I think might be likely to be interested in cultural events. Social media, particularly Facebook, loom large in my promotion strategy. Our library has a small following on Facebook—about 900—but many of them are active followers of the page and learn about our events through this medium. E-mails are sent to all members of the university community, but I also maintain a list of e-mails that have been collected over the years, of people who want to be notified when an event is taking place. Events are also promoted on the radio as well as on local television news programs.

DIPLOMACY AND TACT

Essentially, the goal of someone engaging in diverse types of programming should be to educate and not offend. The role of the librarian in this situation is to bring relevant programming to the audience in a nonthreatening and positive manner. Furthermore, the librarian must be able to diffuse conflicts that may arise during a program in which the topic is controversial. The ability to rephrase potentially offensive remarks so that civil discourse can win out is a valuable skill. It is also worth remembering that some remarks that may seem offensive to people in the audience may stem from ignorance and a lack of direct experience with the topic at hand, so it is important to not leap to the assumption that an apparently inappropriate remark is necessarily intended to be hurtful or derogatory.

GRANT WRITING

It is sometimes difficult to host programming events due to program costs. Frequently, these costs are associated with expenses relating to transportation along with room and board for a guest speaker. One solution to this can be learning to write grants. Before delving into grant writing, it is important to make acquaintances at the university's Sponsored Programs Department. Not only will they assist in making sure all university policies relating to grants are followed, but they will probably have some helpful hints to offer about both grant writing and granting agencies that might be receptive to applications for future library projects. State humanities councils are particularly interested in funding speakers on topics that relate back to their mission. The National Endowment for the Humanities (NEH) as well as the American Library Association (ALA) also regularly make grants available for programming on topics of their choosing. Librarians who are interested in such opportunities should regularly visit their websites. Such grant applications are typically not difficult to complete, certainly not when compared to large, multimillion-dollar grants. The applicant must create a cogent document that fulfills the goals of the grantor, sets forth a realistic plan for programming, and has a budget that is both transparent and that reflects a wise plan for spending the money that is given.

BUDGETING

Budgeting often seems to be one of the more intimidating parts of the programming process, but it is actually a remarkably simple and concrete process.

The grantor is providing a set amount of money, and it is the job of the budget director to spend it as intended by the giving agency. If funds are available, one way that programming librarians can increase their chances of receiving grants, and also have more flexibility in their budgets, is to offer a partial or complete match of the grant amount. Programming grant awards have a tendency to range in amounts of as low as $250 to as high as $10,000. Some of the grants our libraries have received over the years include mini-grants to host guest lectures from the Alabama Humanities Foundation. Their typical award amounts range from $1,000 to $2,000. We also received the Let's Talk About It grant from the ALA and NEH, which provided $4,500 for programming and related travel and expenses. Recently, one of our librarians applied for the ALA and NEH-sponsored programming grant Latino Americans: 500 Years of History, with award amounts of as much as $10,000 for selected institutions. We failed to receive that amount, but we were provided $3,000, which allowed us to have a variety of events celebrating Latino heritage at all three of our libraries.

NETWORKING

Networking is an oft-overused term. However, for programming librarians, particularly those who are engaging in diversity programming, networking can be very important from start to finish. Partnering can be an excellent way "to reach out to patrons and to partner with other groups in the community who have shared goals with the library" (Kern, 2014, 210). In order for a program to be successful, it is important to have partners that have a vested interest in the programming topic. Potential partners are community groups, museums, other libraries, and churches; essentially any organization that would be responsive to the topic being addressed. Such partners offer several benefits. First, and most practical, they potentially provide a natural audience for the programming, because it directly relates to the community they serve. Second, they provide needed insight into the topic being examined through programming, in terms of factual information. Finally, it must be realized that librarianship is a homogenous field that is dominated by whites; partners can assist programming librarians in terms of cultural sensitivity.

Developing partnerships can also have long-term benefits. Once such relationships are solidified, programming librarians often may find that when they conduct events that are not directly related to a specific partner, their members are still in attendance. One of the first partnerships I forged was with a Jewish temple. Their congregants remain the core of all of my activities, whether they are Jewish-themed or not.

CONCLUSION

After six years of intense work as a programming librarian, I have moved into a different role at my library. However, I am glad to see that other librarians at my university have picked up where I left off and are continuing to develop unique, interesting, and culturally diverse programs for our students, faculty, and community at large. When I began hosting such programs, I was the only librarian in our three-library system who was engaging in such activities. In the past year, five librarians at all three locations wrote at least one programming grant that was successful, which is an indication that our engagement with our patrons on this level should continue for some time to come.

REFERENCES

Hanna, Kathleen A., Mindy M. Cooper, and Robin A. Crumrin. 2011. *Diversity Programming and Outreach for Academic Libraries*. Oxford: Chandos.

Kern, Kathleen M. 2014. "What about User Services? Putting the US in RUSA." *Reference & User Services Quarterly* 53, no. 3 (Spring): 209–12.

Leong, Jack Hang Tat. 2013. "Community Engagement—Building Bridges between University and Community by Academic Libraries in the 21st Century." *Libri* 63, no. 3 (September): 220–31.

About the Authors

PATRICIA BANACH recently retired as director of library services at Eastern Connecticut State University where she has served since 2003. She was former cochair of the Connecticut State Colleges and Universities Librarians' Council (2012–2015) and served on its Executive Committee (2014–2016). She also chaired the Connecticut State University Library System Directors Group (2008–2017). She has also served on the Council of Connecticut Academic Library Directors, Vice Chair/Chair Elect 2006 to 2008. Prior to coming to Eastern, she was associate director for collection management at the University of Massachusetts Amherst, where she worked for thirty-one years.

LISA BEINHOFF is currently the managing director of the Texas Tech University Health Sciences Center El Paso Libraries. When she originally drafted this chapter, she was the library director at the New Mexico Institute of Mining and Technology. Beinhoff received both her BFA and her MLS from the University of Illinois at Urbana-Champaign, and she received her PhD in communications from Syracuse University. She has been a regular reviewer for *Choice Magazine* since 1999, and her previous work includes the article entitled, "Library Earthquake Preparedness Planning," which appeared in the *Journal of Library Administration*.

VIRGINIA CAIRNS is currently an instruction librarian at The University of Tennessee at Chattanooga Library. Her background includes management and instruction positions at UT-Chattanooga, Erlanger Health System, and Mercer University.

KIM CLARKE holds a joint appointment as director of the Bennett Jones Law Library and senior lecturer with the faculty of law at the University of Calgary. Previously, she was the assistant dean for library and research services at a private law school in California and worked as the head of the acquisitions department at the Moritz Law Library at The Ohio State University. Her publications include two chapters in *Law Libraries in the Digital Age* (2014) and one in *Beyond the Books: People, Politics and Leadership* (2007).

EMY NELSON DECKER is the NextGen public services manager for the Georgia Tech Library. She holds an MLIS from Valdosta State University and an MA in art history from the University of Chicago. Emy's current interests are centered on reimagining public services toward a greater focus on user engagement and the needs of digital thinkers. In addition to presenting in venues such as the American Library Association and the Association of College & Research Libraries, she has published numerous refereed journal articles and book chapters within the library field. She is also the coeditor of the *Handbook of Research on Disaster Management and Contingency Planning in Modern Libraries*.

BRADFORD LEE EDEN is dean of library services at Valparaiso University. He has a masters and PhD degrees in musicology, as well as an MS in library science. His recent books include *Middle-earth Minstrel: Essays on Music in Tolkien* (2010); *The Associate University Librarian Handbook: A Resource Guide* (2012); *Leadership in Academic Libraries: Connecting Theory to Practice* (2014); *The Hobbit and Tolkien's Mythology: Essays on Revisions and Influences* (2014); and the ten-volume series *Creating the 21st-Century Academic Library* (2015–17). He recently served as president of the Library Publishing Coalition (LPC), and continues to serve on their board of directors.

GARY FITSIMMONS has a BA in communications from Oral Roberts University and an MLS and PhD in library science, both from Texas Woman's University. He has served in academic libraries for 25 of his nearly 27 years in librarianship and as the library director in two academic libraries for 19 years, presently as director of library services for Bryan College (Dayton, Tennessee). Fitsimmons wrote a "Library Leadership" column for *The Bottom Line* journal from 2007 to 2014 and has served as a mentor for aspiring library directors for several years.

SAMANTHA SCHMEHL HINES received her MS in library and information science from University of Illinois in 2003 and has worked in a variety of libraries in many different roles. Currently the associate dean of instructional resources/library director at Peninsula College (Port Angeles, Washington), Hines manages library services for this rural school, focusing on university transfer programs as well as professional/technical training, and supports scholarly issues on campus such as publishing and research ethics. She is a prolific scholar and frequent conference presenter on issues of library services, scholarly communication, and library management. She is the author of *Productivity for Librarians* (2010) and *Revolutionizing the Development of Library and Information Science Professionals* (2014).

THERESA LIEDTKA has served as dean of the library at The University of Tennessee at Chattanooga since 2004. Prior to working at UT-C, she held library positions at California State University Fullerton, Georgetown University (Washington, DC), and Simmons College (Boston, MA). Liedtka has an MLS from Simmons College, an MALS from Georgetown University, and a BA from the University of Massachusetts, Amherst.

JONATHAN MILLER has been the library director at Rollins College (Winter Park, Florida) since 2006, where he is a tenured associate professor and supervises nine other faculty librarians. He earned his MLS from SUNY Buffalo in 1992 and his PhD in information science from the University of Pittsburgh in 2009. He has worked at large research university and small college libraries in Ohio, Illinois, Pennsylvania, and Florida. He has had faculty status at each institution, and supervised faculty librarians at three. His most recent publications can be found at http://bit.ly/1c9YTID.

ELEANOR MITCHELL has been director of library services at Dickinson College since 2005. Prior to that she was head of the undergraduate library at UCLA. Since 2005 she has been coeditor of *Reference Services Review,* a leading professional journal. Eleanor has a strong interest in organizational leadership and change management. She was editor, along with Peggy Seiden, of *Reviewing the Academic Library: A Guide to Self Study and External Review* (2015).

ADAM MURRAY is dean of libraries and educational technologies at James Madison University (Harrisonburg, Virginia) where he has served on a presidential committee focused on community engagement. He previously served as dean of university libraries at Murray State University (Murray, Kentucky) where he was a member of the Town & Gown advisory board. He received his undergraduate degree from the University of North Carolina Wilmington in 2001 and his MILS from The University of North Carolina at Greensboro in

2006. He completed his doctoral degree in 2014 from Western Kentucky University (Bowling Green, Kentucky).

PEGGY SEIDEN has been college librarian at Swarthmore College since 1998. Prior to joining Swarthmore, she directed the Skidmore College Library, the library at Penn State University, New Kensington, and worked in various capacities at Carnegie Mellon University. Her research interests and publications are focused on user behavior, library organizational dynamics, and collaboration. Her most recent publications include *Past or Portal? Enhancing Undergraduate Learning through Special Collections and Archives* (2012), which she coedited with Eleanor Mitchell and Suzy Taraba, and *Reviewing the Academic Library* (2015), which she also coedited with Eleanor Mitchell. Seiden is a past president of ALA's Reference and User Services Association and currently chairs the Choice Editorial Board. She served two terms on the board of PALCI (Pennsylvania Academic Libraries Consortium, Inc.) and was chair in 2010 and 2013. She has an MILS from Rutgers University, a master's degree in mediaeval studies from the University of Toronto, and an undergraduate degree from Colby College.

CHRISTOPHER SHAFFER is dean of Troy University Libraries and has ten years of experience as a librarian. Prior to entering the library field, Shaffer spent eight years as a history teacher in Georgia. He received his MLIS degree from the University of Alabama in 2005 and his EdD in educational leadership, policy, and law from Alabama State University in 2014. He has been published in several journals, has considerable experience writing and implementing grants, and has presented nationally.

PAT TULLY has worked in academic libraries since she was hired as a student assistant at Cape Cod Community College in 1982. Since receiving her MILS in 1988 from the University of Michigan, she has held a series of increasingly responsible positions in public and academic libraries, first in technical services and then in administration. She worked at Wesleyan University Library for five years as associate university librarian, and then, starting in 2009, as university librarian. Tully is now director of the Ketchikan Public Library (Alaska).

Index